D0117008

Tim Darling

How to Get Into the Top Consulting Firms:
A Surefire Case Interview Method

SECOND EDITION

intaglio publishing

Copyright © 2009 by Tim Darling
PUBLISHED BY INTAGLIO PUBLISHING

Library of Congress Cataloging-in-Publication Data
ISBN 0-615-27989-9

All rights to illustrations and text reserved by the author. This work may not be copied, reproduced, or translated in whole or in part without written permission of the author, except for brief excerpts in connection with reviews or scholarly analysis. Use with any form of information storage and retrieval, electronic adaptation or otherwise, or by similar or dissimilar methods is also strictly forbidden without written permission of the author.

Printed in the United States of America   *Second edition, second printing, June 2009*

Contents

To my wife, Ellie

1   Introduction

Outstanding problem-solving is the core skill that all consultants bring to their clients. Problem-solving is the process of outlining a clear path to a solution and then focusing on the key salient facts that are necessary for maneuvering down that path. Other qualities – such as being able to empathize with a client's situation or to bring a fresh and unbiased perspective – are important, but only as they support the process of arriving at a solution. So it is no coincidence that raw problem-solving skills are the heart of what firms look for when administering case interviews.

The primary reason that I wrote this book is that I believed too many candidates were focusing on memorizing isolated prescribed solutions for case interviews at the expense of demonstrating their own problem-solving talents. While no one needs to invent unique solutions for every problem on every occasion, in at least one part of every case interview, attempt to say something along the lines of: "I've never seen a problem like this before, but here's how I would think about approaching it…"

If the interviewer leaves the interview without having seen a good insight into your own individual abilities to attack problems, it's easy to imagine that they may have a tough time recommending the advance of your candidacy.

What are the firms looking for?

The interviewers are simply asking themselves: Would I want this person on my team? If I give them a few facts and point them in the right direction, can they run with it? Are they fun and interesting? Will they be a positive force in the team room? Will they make me and my team *better*?

Case interviews are one way of helping to make that decision. The interviewer will hand you a nebulous problem – as your team leaders might do on the first day of a study – and watch you disaggregate its key drivers. They want to see if you can do a reasonably deep level of analysis on each component and are then able to synthesize your findings into an articulate CEO-level recommendation. This entire process often takes associates over a year to fully master, but the case interview is a good litmus test to see if you have the foundation to be a good associate.

Enjoying cases is similarly a good litmus test for you to see if consulting is a good career choice for you. You should have fun practicing and preparing for them! Case interviews are like crossword puzzles. They may be challenging, but after you've done a few, your confidence should grow and you should begin to enjoy them.

What does this book have that other case interview books don't?

There are many good resources available for students interviewing with consulting firms. Consulting clubs at most business schools have collections of cases to practice on, workshops about the interview process, as well as advice and mentorship from other students who have been through the process. In addition to that, simply practicing cases with a few different people is your best option to become an expert interviewee.

While this book is just another element in the mix, it is different from most other preparation books for the following reasons:

- This book was written by a consultant at a top firm who also interviewed with a number of other consulting firms.
- This book articulates what firms are really looking for and demonstrates how you can develop those skills (quickly and easily) instead of just listing structures that you need to memorize.
  - Personally, I found some of the other books about case interviews to be overwhelming: they typically either have many large independent structures to memorize or they don't have any central idea that ties everything together.
- This book is holistic. Instead of just looking at case interviews, it looks at the entire lifecycle from fine-tuning your résumé to contributing to a team problem-solving session on the first day of your first engagement.
- It is a quick read. My goal is to give you the best, most critical insights I can in the most synthesized and efficient way possible. I could have made this book much longer, but after the first couple of hours, your time is better spent practicing cases than reading about them.
- Finally, this is one man's approach to the interview process and to being a consultant. I hope that it will provide you with some of the most useful tools that you'll acquire. Don't follow the suggestions word-for-word; instead, consider adopting ideas you discover here and elsewhere into your own style. This book should be complementary to the other resources and methods available to you. If you find that the Valuation Framework in Chapter 6 helps you approach many of the popular case types, then you should make use of it. At the very least, hopefully it will give you some ideas and provide a foundation for critical analysis and discussion.

What's new in this second edition?

I wrote the first draft of this book after finishing my summer internship with a top consulting firm. I shared it with a number of my fellow students who were interviewing for full-time positions in the fall and later heard from them that it was a key element in their interview preparation and subsequent success.

I now have about a year's worth of full-time consulting experience to draw from and this edition is an update that reflects that. Perhaps surprisingly, my interest in case interviews is stronger now than ever. I have only recently begun to appreciate a good case interview as a full microcosm of business strategy and problem-solving: very few 30 minute dialogues can match it as a vehicle for creativity and richness of thought.

The approaches that are included here have grown and developed over time to include new ideas that I've encountered – though the fundamentals have remained consistent. Specifically, this second edition includes some of the key ideas about how to value a company or investment based on the principles in McKinsey & Company's book, *Valuation: Measuring and Managing the Value of Companies*. The valuation approach builds neatly off of the profit tree given in the first edition and opens up a lot of new avenues for other case types to build from. We can consider any investment decision through the valuation lens, though by far the most popular investment case types are new product introduction and competitor acquisition. An overview of the details of valuation, which is beyond what you need to know for case interviews, is included in Appendix 2. I also recommend the *Valuation* book if you are interested in details of this approach.

Over the last year or so I've also received a lot of feedback on the original text. I've tried to account for most of them here in the updates I've made. Most of the feedback I've received has been in comparing this book to Marc Cosentino's popular case preparation book, *Case In Point*. I personally see this book as a complement to Cosentino's and not a competitor. His book takes a different perspective and I believe most candidates would benefit from seeing both. As one student suggested to me recently, Cosentino's book can be thought of as presenting the art of case interviews while this one presents the science of them.

2   *Do you want to be a consultant?*

Asking "do you want to be a consultant?" may sound like a funny question to pose at the start. But I've met a couple of people who joined consulting firms without asking why they wanted to join, did well, got promoted, and then realized that it wasn't a good fit for them. So if they could have benefited from someone asking them why they wanted to go into consulting early on, I'm sure others could too.

Consulting has a lot of positive qualities, but it's not for everyone. The people you'll work with in a consulting firm may be some of the smartest and hardest-working people you'll ever meet. You'll naturally compare yourself to them, set their level as your baseline, and push yourself to meet their standards. You may be performing on an extraordinary level for many months but believe that you're just clocking in at an average pace because the bar is so high. In other words, if you're used to being a star performer at work and are accustomed to receiving that level of attention, you may have to adjust your expectations.

There will also probably be another transition when you leave consulting and move on to the next step in your career. You might be surprised to find that the people you work with in the future might not pick up and run with your ideas as quickly and they may be less enthusiastic about pushing new innovations if it means they have to work past 5PM on any given night.

What is a consultant's lifestyle like?

There is no average lifestyle. It varies a lot by firm, office location, travel arrangement, and engagement. Travel and time commitment varies greatly between firms, office location, and engagement.

On one engagement at one firm, consultants may work 8AM-8PM Monday to Thursday and 9-5 on Friday with spikes for deliverables. On another, they may travel on Monday and Thursday and work until midnight on Monday, Tuesday, and Wednesday nights. For some firms, consultants do most of their work at the client; for others, the team may only visit the client once a week.

You should have some time every day to exercise and read or watch a few minutes of TV. In addition, each study may have two to three times where you may work most of the night to get a deliverable ready for a big meeting the next day.

Travel can be tiring: both in the physical sense and in the emotional sense of leaving your house and family or pets for three to five days per week. Some consulting firms let you work from your home office and you may sometimes have in-town assignments. If you are working out of New York or London offices, for example, the majority of your work may require no travel, but you may work longer hours due to the nature of the clients. As you consider different firms, ask the representatives from them about their experiences with travel, the average number of hours, and the variability of lifestyle over different engagements.

How do you ensure a healthy lifestyle?

The travel, room service / restaurant food, and the long sedentary work can have adverse health effects. Exercise and eating well are important. Equally vital is being able to combat stress by taking control of your lifestyle as much as you can and keeping your eye on the big picture. Why are you really on the engagement? Why are you in consulting? Having a plan for your day and your career can help with this.

One key element of staying physically and emotionally well-balanced is to set boundaries and enforce them. At the beginning of your study, it's up to you to tell your team leadership that you won't work on weekends and that you need to talk to your family on the phone at 10PM every night from your hotel room. Maybe you need an hour's exercise every day or seven hours' sleep Monday through Wednesday. (Thursday through Sunday nights you should naturally have more control over your schedule.) You can't have everything you want, but if you pick your battles, you should be able to have what's most important to you. Most critically, it's up to you – not your teams' leaders – to enforce your boundaries once you've gotten your team to buy into them.

What type of person is most successful as a consultant?

There's a wide range of diversity in consulting firms in personality types and backgrounds. One element that seems to be consistent across most successful members of top firms is a high degree of energy. People who tend to do well usually don't mind working long hours on tough problems at a fast pace, dealing with multiple obstacles at once on multiple parts of a workstream, sometimes not getting enough sleep, and being raced from one location to another by all modes of transportation – all while keeping a smile on their face and the spirits of their team high. But the truth is that everyone gets tired and has to take some time off; many people leave after 18 months simply because they don't have the energy or willpower to keep moving at the required pace.

Consulting can be tough sometimes, but in my experience, it's one of the most rewarding learning experiences that you can sign up for. The key to being successful at it and being happy is to understand your lifestyle needs, draw boundaries that reflect them, and enforce those boundaries when your engagements get busy.

3   Résumés

The first step in landing a job at a consulting firm is to get past the résumé screen. Exhibit 3-1 shows an example résumé which is simply offered as a point of reference. The objective for your résumé is two-fold: to get the interview and to give the interviewer a reference to ask questions during the interview.

To meet the first goal, you should highlight the skills that the firms are looking for: leadership, communication skills, and similar. For the second goal, highlight the stories that you want to talk about in the interview.

Content guidelines

- Use quantifiable metrics when referring to your accomplishments. If you can claim that the work you led or did had a specific effect, then mention it.
- Use strong action words: led, coordinated, invented, or similar.
- One good format is: "<High-level accomplishment> by <action>", such as: "Increased product revenue by 4% by leading a major new advertising campaign."
- Be executive summary-oriented and talk about the actual results of your work. Read over each accomplishment on your résumé and ask: how would your boss or your boss's boss view this? They would likely be less concerned with the specific details ("wrote 100,000 lines of code") and more interested in the net result of your work ("increased customer base by 6% with a new internet distribution channel").
- Your claims have to be believable or easily provable. If you claim to have single-handedly reduced your last employer's costs by 15% but don't offer any supporting evidence for it, the reviewer may well be skeptical.

> **Choose fewer words, but better chosen ones. Your résumé should feel more like an advertisement for you than a page from your autobiography.**

- Pick the extracurricular activities that you list at the bottom of the page carefully. Choose ones that tie to stories that you'd like to tell. Often during an interview, an interviewer will glance over your résumé, find something that looks interesting, and ask for more detail. You want the items that catch their eye to be the ones that you have the most interesting stories to support.

| xxx Oak St
Sioux City, IA 51106 | **Jim Starling** | 712-xxx-xxxx
xxx@stlukes.edu |

Education

| 2007–2009 | WILLIAMS SCHOOL OF BUSINESS, ST LUKE'S UNIVERSITY | Sioux City, IA |

M.B.A.

- Merit scholarship (2007-2009).
- Concentrations: Finance and Strategy.
- GMAT: 720 (92%).

| 1996–2000 | UNIVERSITY OF ILLINOIS, URBANA-CHAMPAIGN | Champaign, IL |

B.S., Economics & Computer Science

- Illinois Scholarship (1999); Dean's List; GPA: 3.6.
- Honors Thesis: *The Effect of the Internet on Developing Economies.*

Experience

| 1/2007–
8/2007 | JEFFERSON VOLUNTEERS | Lexington, KY |

Co-Founder

- Co-founded a group of 120 undergraduates who each dedicate 5 hours a week to community volunteering.

| 5/2004–
8/2007 | GEAR-O-MATIC GROUP (a Fortune 1000 toy manufacturer) | Lexington, KY |

Manager (2005-2007); Analyst (2004-2005)

- **Thought leadership:** Invented a major production system that decreased factory floor costs by 12% and factory line turnaround time by 22% (2005).
- **Communication:** Presented strategic plan to VPs and received $2.5MM in funding.
- Led a team of 4 in proposing and implementing plan.
- United 50+ employees from varying departments to build marketing plan.
- **Teamwork:** Served on a dozen committees to improve cross-functional communication.

| 5/2002–
3/2004 | PRESTON SECURITIES | Washington, DC |

Financial Analyst, Acquisitions Group

- Invested the impact of M&A activities based on market research, NPV analyses, and comparables.
- **C-level presentation:** Conducted research on the trends of international currencies and presented results to members of the firm's executive management team.

Additional Info

- Avid skier; placed 3rd in International Alpine Competition (Geneva, 1999).
- Member, American Polo Club.
- Fluent in French with an interest in learning new languages.

Exhibit 3-1 Sample résumé

- Start key bullet entries with a bold word/phrase that tells the reviewer what that entry represents. For example, the entry "Led team of 5 in operational analysis" could imply leadership, operations knowledge, or analytical skills. Most entries will display multiple qualities, but if you intended that entry to show a strong example of leadership, explicitly tag it as such. Another benefit of this is you can find out the top five qualities that the company you're interviewing for is interested in and choose your tags to reflect those qualities. For example, the applicant in Exhibit 3-1 highlights "thought leadership", "communication," and "teamwork".
  - Enumerate the top three traits that you want to convey with your résumé and then look at each line item on your résumé and ask which area it contributes to.
  - Is the message that you want to convey obvious or could a reviewer interpret the item differently? If so, you might consider rewording the item or start the line with a keyword.
- Can you convey the message more simply? For example, if you are listing the five clubs that you belong to as a student to convey "impact", would it be more effective to simply write: "Active member of 5 student clubs?" Or if you wish to convey leadership: "Served as a VP of 2 student clubs that represent over 1,000 unique student members combined." Consider any list in your résumé, such as a list of publications, memberships, awards, or achievements in this context. Don't rely too heavily on the readers' ability to interpret lengthy lists of activities as evidence of any specific quality.
- If you know the reviewers are interested in GPA or GMAT scores (or similar) and yours is within the ballpark of their target range, include it. If you're above the 90th percentile on standardized tests, consider including the percentile too.
- What are your three biggest and most impressive accomplishments? If you hand your résumé to someone, can they spot those three things in fifteen seconds or less? What is the one most unique thing that you've ever done? Does it similarly stand out? Having accomplished twenty impressive items in your career and listing them all may cause a reviewer to gloss over most of them. See if you can synthesize two or more entries into one line.
  - Prioritize entries by moving them to the top of each set of bullets. If you really want their eye to go straight to any particular entry, bold part of it, although it's best not to overuse typeface changes.
- If you worked for a company that they may not be familiar with, consider adding a short description, such as the "Fortune 1000 toy manufacturer" line in Exhibit 3-1.

Visual guidelines

- Keep the Education and Experience header lines in a relatively small and unassuming font so that the reviewer's eyes don't focus on them at a first glance. They should not attract attention away from the content.

- Use the small caps option in Microsoft Word and a bold font for the headers of each sub-section: the names of your previous universities and employers. This is where the reviewers' eyes should immediately go to.

- Make every effort to synthesize your accomplishments into a single page résumé, especially if you have less than five years of previous work experience. Being able to condense large amounts of data into a succinct story is a key skill for new consultants; having a single page résumé is your first step in demonstrating that you can do that.

- Months and 4-digit dates for each entry ("1/2007") are easiest to read. Keep all dates on either the far left or far right side of the page so that it's easy to check how many years of total work experience you have.

- White space is valuable: no one will read hundreds of words on a résumé. Hand your résumé to someone and ask them to read it. Stop them after thirty seconds: how far did they get? A reviewer likely won't spend more than thirty seconds to a minute reading your résumé. 10 to 12 point font and 2 to 4 bullet points per heading are good general rules.

- Write "led team of 3" instead of "led team of three". It is more likely to catch the reader's eye.

- If you can keep each bullet point to one line, it makes them easier to read. See the sample résumé in Exhibit 3-1: which bullet points are you more likely to read? Probably the GMAT line – it's so short and succinct that it's impossible to miss.

4   Networking and mixers/office hours/pre-interviews

Office hours are events where a group of representatives from the company will be available for an informal conversation. Mixers are similar events for you and the firms to get to know each other and are typically held at a bar or restaurant. These are usually only for applicants who are currently in MBA or undergraduate programs.

These events are typically screenings for interviews. Dress well (always overdress if in doubt), go early and stay late, speak clearly and articulately enough to be easily heard, smile, be polite, and listen attentively to what the representatives are saying. As they talk, think of interesting follow-ups to keep the conversation moving with a natural flow. Don't try to crack jokes. This is a time to show your best professional self; it's not the time to be overly social.

When you meet a representative from the company at an event, shake hands and look them in the eye. Say your name clearly. Have a few questions ready ahead of time but try to keep the atmosphere of the talk at a comfortable conversation level and not a disconnected barrage of pre-scripted questions.

Go with the honest goal of trying to learn more about what they do and what makes their organization special. Don't ask questions that you know the answer to just so you can say something. Ask about the good and the bad. No job is perfect and it's valuable to know what areas they have found difficult.

Treat everyone professionally, respectfully, and politely, but don't change how you interact with the representatives based on their age or tenure with the firm. Partners are people too (as are the Fortune 500 CEOs with whom you may eventually be working with!) and it is always okay to treat human beings as human beings. Be friendly; ask them how their day is going.

Don't block other potential candidates' ability to interact with the visitors by crowding them or asking more than your share of questions. Meet everyone in the room if you can. When you move on, say thanks and ask if they have a business card. Have your business cards available in case they ask for one. Later that night, send an email thanking them for coming, mention one thing you discussed, and reiterate your interest in their firm. Don't wait more than a couple of hours to send the email if possible: they will likely make their decisions about whom to invite for interviews later that night and a polite follow-up thank you notes could have an influence in their decision.

Be respectful of the representatives' time when emailing them. The best email might be to simply thank them for visiting and to say how excited you are about their organization. They'll appreciate not having to spend a lot of time replying especially if you're only asking them because you think you have to ask something.

5　Interviews (general advice)

Interviewers – for consulting firms or anywhere else – have one simple goal: to decide if the person they're interviewing could make their team and their company better. The interviewer will ask themselves things like: is this someone I'd want on my study? Is this someone I'd want as an officemate? Is this someone who can challenge my thinking and give me a new perspective on any particular issue or life in general?

Imagine two different applicants. One is really fast with the numbers but isn't very friendly, enthusiastic, or interesting to talk to. The other is the opposite. If the interviewer had the first person assigned to join their team, they'd do great work with little coaching. The second would need more coaching and attention, but they're so compassionate and energetic that spending an hour a day mentoring them would be fun. Who would get the job? It will obviously depend on many other factors, but you can imagine the second person would at least have a good chance.

The point is that there are a lot of smart people who don't get every job they apply for: sheer intelligence and depth of experience are just two elements in the mix. Other elements, such as the ability to win over other people may even be more important. How can you acquire and effectively use these "people elements"? Be excited, enthusiastic, honest, warm, calm, confident, and relaxed. How can you do those things? There are a few ways, but the most important is to smile.

Smile! And a few other suggestions

One of the most important qualities that you can bring to an interview or a consulting engagement is the ability to relax other people and create an atmosphere of trust and harmony. Smile like you're enjoying yourself and you really like the person that you're talking to. Smile like you're confident and in full control of the situation. It's the easiest thing to do and can have a huge impact.

After that, respond enthusiastically to questions. For example, a response to "how are you?" such as "I'm excellent!" catches people by surprise and makes them want to hang around you to see if it will rub off on them. Just make sure you say it for real; you don't want to sound sarcastic. If your interviewer likes you, they'll be more likely to want to help you or overlook some of your shortcomings.

Be positive

Be positive when talking about past jobs and co-workers. Be positive when discussing past business problems you've run into or some of your weaknesses, if asked. Being able to take tough situations and difficult people and turn them into fun challenges is a great quality to bring to a consulting team.

Don't complain about the weather, your flight, or the toughness of the case. Interviewers respond well to positive energy and you want them to like you immediately.

Win them over early on. The walk from the waiting room to the interview room may be the most important thirty seconds in your interview. Engage them; establish a connection or something in common. If nothing else, be excited, happy, and enthusiastic. Your interviewers probably don't want to be there any more than you do. Reward them for making the sacrifice in their day to interview you. Imagine that they're a client who is paying a lot of money to bring you in.

Maintain confidence, calmness, and give the impression that you're always in control. Everyone has at least one moment where they find themselves out of their depth when discussing topics that they're not very comfortable with or answering questions for which they are not completely sure of the answer. Believe in what you're saying, sound as if you know what you're doing, and gain their trust by keeping your composure. Don't let your frustrations or anxiety show. This advice is just as important when you're a consultant meeting with a client as it is in interviews.

Keep the entire interview feeling like one long continuous conversation

Try to maintaining a conversational feel throughout the entire interview. This can be tough to do because there are defined segments where you have to switch between with little segue.

Interviews often have a behavioral section, a case, and time for you to ask questions. Making the behavioral interview feel like a conversation (where you're doing most of the talking) just takes a little practice. Tell interesting stories and occasionally give them a pause to jump in if they want to follow up on something that caught their attention. Tie stories from your past back to the company you're interviewing with to keep the conversation relevant and current.

Maintaining the conversational flow in the case interview and in the gaps between the interview segments can be tough. One way is to occasionally inject some of your own experiences. For example, consider a case where you have suggested a customer loyalty program as one way of increasing volume. You can step out of the case for a minute and talk about how you, as a customer, have viewed loyalty programs in similar stores; are they positive or negative experiences? Why? This adds a new angle to a case the interviewer may have given many times and engages them in an interesting discussion that transcends the case.

Be prepared

Learn everything you reasonably can about the company. Visiting their website and at least reading the section on how to prepare for interviews with them (if they have one) should be a bare minimum. Talking to current or former employees about their experiences is valuable, even if just to mention in your interview or cover letter that you did so. Such insight will help you ask a few good questions at the end of the interview too.

Have an elevator pitch about yourself. What's the 30-second reason that they should hire you?

Ask the interviewer questions at the end of the interview

After the behavioral and case interviews, the last component of an interview is when you get to ask questions of the interviewer. Here again, it's important to start a conversation and keep it flowing. Don't just have three unrelated questions to ask. Start with a big open-ended question or follow up with something mentioned earlier in the interview. The goal is not to extract information from them like they're an ATM; it's to establish a comfortable and natural rapport where you're conversing like peers. You have these types of conversations with other people every day, so it shouldn't be that hard. Just be professional and remember that it's up to you to build a meaningful connection. Listen to their responses and always be considering how you could follow up: do you want to clarify something, dive deeper in one area, side step into a related idea, or perhaps add something from your own experience?

Ask questions that will help you better decide if their organization would be a good fit for you. After talking to many representatives from their firm at various events and previous interviews, you may reach a point where you no longer have any questions. But as you interview with higher-level leaders in successive rounds, the types of insight that they may be able to give you can be very different from the insight given by consultants who have only been working for a few months or a few years.

Consulting firms adapt to industry trends; they sometimes even lead those changes. Once you have a solid understanding of the firm as it currently exists, think about it as a dynamic organization that will change during your time working there. Ask the representatives of the firm questions that will help you visualize what those changes are likely to be.

For example:

- What is the rate of change of industry mix in the firm overall in the last three to five years?
  - Has the organization entered new industries or left others?
  - Why has it been changing?
    - ("Why has x occurred?" is a good format for follow-up questions in general.)

Prepare for this part of the interview. Put thought ahead of time into finding questions that you are legitimately interested in the answers to.

Interviews are a two-way decision process. They are for you and the organizations to determine if there's a mutually good fit. As you think about questions to ask during the interview process, consider questions that will help you determine if the firms that you interview with will be places that you would like to work. Whatever questions you decide to ask, ideally you should be able to leave each interview with a better insight into critical decision factors such as:

- Do you share the firm's values?
- Can you imagine working with your interviewers on a daily basis?
- Did they treat you courteously?
- Do the people you meet look enthusiastic, happy, and engaged?
  - Did your interviewer give you their full attention during the interview or did they spend time checking their Blackberry? What do those types of clues tell you about how the organization operates?
- If money and prestige weren't factors, would you accept the job?

6 *Case interviews*

Executive summary

Fundamentally, all businesses share the same objective: to create value for their share-holders, usually by making money now and in the future. Ideally, they do this by creating value in a stable market and then strategically positioning themselves to be able to sustainably keep as much of that value as possible (by keeping competitors, suppliers, customers, and the government from taking too much of it away).

Case interviews are simplified abstractions of situations that highlight fundamental business objectives and the external forces that drive and influence them. Case interviews are often reenactments of the consultant/CEO partnership where you, as the interviewee, are playing the role of the consultant.

In a case interview, you may step into a corporation that is considering introducing a ground-breaking new product. Or your client may be considering entering an existing market with a product line that's new to them. Or you may join the story a few years later, when a once-successful company has seen a decrease in profits. In all of these cases, your goal is to determine if there's an opportunity to generate or increase profits, suggest a plan of action to capitalize on that opportunity, and illuminate the possible risks and market reactions to your plan.

While there are many different types of issues that a corporation may face (and thus many different types of case interviews), all of them ultimately reduce to the same fundamental objective: to create value by generating profits.[a] And so the profit tree (revenue minus costs and all of the sub-trees underneath those two drivers) is the centerpiece of the Valuation Framework introduced later in this chapter. Sometimes it will be a subcomponent of your case, such as with mergers or acquisitions. Other times, your case will focus on a small subcomponent of the tree, such as a case to change the distribution channels – and thus improve fixed costs.

---

[a] A slight qualification may be needed here. Many firms, especially consulting and other private or professional firms, put serving customer needs as their top goal; profitability is simply a side effect of doing that well. Other firms have secondary objectives, such as to be responsible citizens. But no business will survive if it doesn't consistently make profit-generating decisions. So whether those decisions were initially made for profitability reasons or not, valuing all decisions through the lens of income potential is a valuable step. And as discussed in Appendix 1, firms should also only make major investment decisions in ways that directly help move them towards a single specific strategic goal. The only other qualification that may be needed is that non-profits may have other ways of "creating value" other than profitability; therefore it is important to clarify the client's objective early on in the discussion. (Additionally, a CPA might also add that businesses have two other financial goals: to maintain a positive cash flow and to keep the firm in good financial condition through prudent management of assets and liabilities.)

But while the profit tree itself is usually relevant in some form, it only represents the surface of the machine. The power in using it lies in your understanding of its moving parts and the external market forces that can influence those parts, such as customers, competitors, and suppliers.

The two principal goals of this chapter are to discuss methods for inventing your own tree structures in a case and to introduce the Valuation Framework. In the latter case, we'll also discuss the moving parts and forces that influence it and provide you with the tools to build a coherent conversation around these elements that will help lead you to a solution.

STOP! Try practicing a case or two before reading any further...

If you have never practiced a case interview and/or have a limited business background, try practicing a case or two with a partner before proceeding. Cases #1 and #2 in Chapter 10 may be good options.

It's only after you get a sense of the dynamics and challenges in a case interview that you'll be able to constructively evaluate how well different methods, such as the ones presented here, could work for you. Only once you have an idea of what you do well (and where you have trouble) will you have the context to learn new tips and tools. The purpose of this book is to build an overall approach to solving problems in a back-of-the-envelope, 30-minute, case-style format and to do that effectively requires a little bit of context and experience with case interviews.

If you have trouble figuring out how to approach your first few cases, don't worry. You should struggle with the cases that you practice early on. Case #1 in Chapter 10 also has a sample set of notes and structure that you can compare your page of notes to after going through the case to help diagnose your methods and to consider ideas for future improvement. Skimming Chapter 7 at this point may also help give you some insights.

In addition, if you don't have a business background, consider reading Appendix 1 for an overview on strategy and how it shapes and informs business decisions, such as the ones that you will encounter in case interviews.

Summary of the case interview process and some general tips

The interviewer will quickly describe the company and the situation that your case will revolve around. Start by articulating the main objective of the case (uncover ways to increase profits, determine cause of revenue decline, decide whether to introduce a new product, or similar). If it's not obvious why the company wants to accomplish the given objective, then ask. If applicable, also ask the interviewer to quantify the objective.

Next, it's often helpful to step back and ask a high level question about what the company's products or services are. This will give you insight into whether you should investigate profitability at a product level or for the entire organization, for example.

Then write the objective at the top of your paper, ask for a minute to collect your thoughts, and build a MECE tree out underneath the objective.

"MECE" is a consulting term meaning "mutually exclusive and collectively exhaustive" (pronounced "mee-see"). When you divide something into smaller pieces, do you miss any part or do you count a part more than once? A MECE structure divides an issue into non-overlapping parts that cover the complete issue space. This tree should break the main issue into a collection of smaller and more manageable subcomponents. The tree will tell you what you need to investigate and what questions to ask; you should be able to follow the tree directly to the solution.

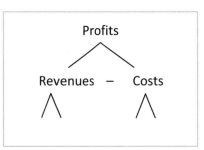

Exhibit 6-1 A basic profit tree

As mentioned earlier, a popular tree for disaggregating profits breaks it into revenues and costs, as shown in Exhibit 6-1. As you follow the revenue sub-tree down one or two more levels, customers and competitors enter as forces that can affect your prices, costs, and volume. Suppliers enter as forces that affect your costs and perhaps limit your volume. Given a good structure, the solution to the case – such as that supplier consolidation has increased your cost base and thus decreased your profits – will naturally unravel.

Find the right balance of structure, creativity, and flexibility

Case interviews require a balance of structure, creativity, and flexibility, as shown in Exhibit 6-2. Interviewers are looking for unique approaches and creative insights shared in a structured format. You also have to be able to adjust or refocus your structure as the interviewer leads you in specific directions.

Creativity means moving beyond the standard frameworks (if you use them) or creating your own unique framework for attacking a problem. You can also be creative by pulling in insights from other industries or your own previous experiences in a way that differentiates you from other candidates.

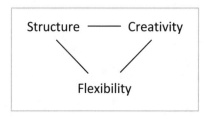

Exhibit 6-2 The case interview triangle

Structure is the main message of this book. Structured problem-solving ensures that you consider all possible elements to a problem and attack it in a systematic and logical manner. There is a natural tension between structure and creativity but it is possible to demonstrate both qualities at different points in the interview.

The final element is *flexibility*. This is the ability to tailor or refocus your approach based on either the interviewer's preferences or on new information that becomes available. If the interviewer's own preferred approach is different from yours, they will likely ask some questions about your structure to test its soundness but then give hints to focus your efforts in a particular area, perhaps because the data needed to use your approach is not available. For example, if you use a valuation-based approach for a case where the objective is to decide whether or not to acquire a competitor (such as the Valuation Framework in Exhibit 6-6), you might propose comparing the premium that we'd pay for the target with the additional value that we'd expect to create through the acquisition. Because there are many other ways to approach an M&A case, the interviewer may not have these exact data points.

Being flexible does not necessarily mean scrapping your approach and adopting a completely different one. If your structure is clear and complete, following it will lead you to the solution and you should feel confident in doing so.

A little bit of practice will help you find the right balance between these three qualities that may at first appear to be somewhat in conflict with each other.

Start with a few sheets of plain white paper…

- Write on the plain white paper in landscape format.
- Start by drawing a line down the left quarter of the paper (about 3 inches from the left edge).
- Write your notes from the beginning of the case in that margin. If you draw a margin to take notes in, then the space limitation immediately requires you to develop the good habit of synthesizing key facts into short entries.
  - For example, consider a case where the interviewer says, "your client is a regional retail bank; they serve only consumers, not businesses. Profits are down. We want to increase profits by \$3 million over the next years. What levers can we pull to grow?" Your paper may then look like this:

Regional bank
Consumers, not businesses
$\pi \downarrow$
Obj: $\uparrow \pi$ \$3M / 3 yrs
<u>What levers to pull?</u>

Exhibit 6-3 An example of a candidate's early case notes

- Practice writing in shorthand: use the Greek pi (π) for profits and arrows for increasing or decreasing. Make sure your shorthand will be understandable by the interviewer. They may try to read your notes during the case and they may collect them after the interview is over.
- Try to write out the full objective as much as possible. You don't want to look at it later on and wonder what you initially meant by certain abbreviations.
  - ◻ Circle or underline the objective. At the end of the case, knowing exactly where your initial notes are and what the objective is will be very important: your "summary to the CEO" should start with a quick summary of the objective.
- Quantify the objectives. If the interviewer says, "we want to increase profits", ask if there's a target: how much and by when? Ideally, there should be some numbers in this margin. If the case is about a venture capital firm that is considering investing in a company, what level of returns do they expect? Once you have quantified the objectives, ask for a sense of perspective to better understand how achievable they are. Is $3 million a 10% increase or 30%?
- Once you have your notes, summarize them for the interviewer to verify that you heard everything correctly.
- In many cases, it's also a good idea to ask one or two general questions to get to know the client and the industry. It's almost always valuable to ask what their products are.
  - ◻ Put the product names toward the bottom of the page, just to the right of the line. Leave room to the right of the products' names for a table where you can take notes on product margins or market share for each product. If you build a profit tree for the entire company, it may be valuable to know that some products are more profitable than others.
- Often, a question worth asking is, "why are we doing this?"
  - ◻ Often this will be obvious (such as to increase profits), but it may be less obvious for acquisition cases: is the acquisition a defensive move against a competitor, for example? Do we want to reduce costs due to competitor pressures or to give ourselves more strategic options? Another question that may be useful in cases to increase profits is to ask "where do our profits come from?" Do 80% of our profits come from a few customers? Do 80% of our profits come from one product?

Don't get caught up in the details. Consider the case as an abstract business issue.

- A common mistake is to make assumptions about the company or the industry based on past knowledge and to not verify them with the interviewer.
  - The first step in avoiding this is to recognize any assumptions that you're making. Be especially careful if you're familiar with the industry that you're discussing.
- Ask the interviewer for a minute to collect your thoughts and then use the rest of the right side of the paper to build your structure / framework tree and to take additional notes and do calculations throughout the case.
- At the top of the right side of you paper, in the center of the page, write the objective and then build your structure beneath it.
- Once you've built your approach, share it with the interviewer in 20-30 seconds. Practice being concise: give an overview of the objective and the 2-3 main drivers that you will consider. Then, for each main driver, quickly list off the subdrivers. Then pause and read the interviewer to get a sense of whether you should explain any of them in more detail or start to focus you attention on one of them.
- Finally, be flexible. Your structure may be a good approach but not the one that they had in mind. Listen for their lead and be willing to take a different approach if needed.

There are many ways to get to the right answer…

There is no one right way to solve any particular problem. Granted, in this book, I present many suggestions and opinions. The Valuation Framework is an example of that: it's my preferred way of thinking about business problems. While I believe it's a coherent way of approaching cases, it is certainly not the only way or the "right" way. Other case interview guides and resources will offer other approaches, as will other people whom you practice cases with. Ultimately the only right way to solve a problem is the one that makes the most sense to you and allows you to consistently arrive at a solution.

…and to demonstrate that, I'll give a critique of a practice case on a top firm's website

I stepped through an online case on a consulting firm's website recently[a] and was disappointed at not only how rigid the online format is at allowing creative responses, but also at how the online case defined its "correct" approach at the expense of other options. I imagine any prospective candidate could be very disheartened by practicing one of these

---

[a] You can take the case yourself. I took it in March 2009 on joinbain.com's Interview Preparation website. It's "Practice Case I: Personal Care Co.".

online cases and discovering that their method (which may have worked well for them) is "wrong" in the eyes of their potential employer! So let me be a voice that says that you should take any advice you receive – whether it's from me, another book, or a consulting firm's website – with a healthy dose of skepticism. Pressure-test new ideas with the reference point of your own knowledge, creativity, and experiences.

To illustrate this point, I'll give a quick overview of the beginning steps in this particular online case and argue why the proposed reasoning given is either incorrect or at least not the only correct approach.

The objective that the online case presents is: "Our client, Private Equity Co. (PEC), is looking to acquire Personal Care Co." The initial question it asks is: "how would you go about breaking this problem down?" Then the following options are given:

- Competitor analysis
- Customer / market attractiveness
- Company attractiveness
- Legal issues
- Potential synergies
- Growth projection

If you adopt a version of the framework proposed in this book, then the top items in your structure might include:

- Standalone value of the target
- - Purchase price
- + Additional value we can create (through synergies, better management, …)
- Cultural/legal barriers

This is perfectly reasonable top-level approach. Implicit in it is this dialgoue: They should make the acquisition if: (1) the value of the firm's outstanding shares *minus* the price we have to pay to acquire them *plus* any additional value that we can create, in total, is significantly large and (2) there are no legal or cultural barriers that will threaten the acquisition. The phrase "significantly large" reflects the consideration that there is a cost to the capital that we need to invest; capital is a constrained resource that we could also use in other opportunities.

The three options on the right (legal, synergies, growth projection) best fit this approach, although they are not a perfectly good fit. Still, they are arguably relevant. But if you choose them, you will learn that you're 0-for-3: the proposed solution are the three on the left: Customers, Competitors, and Company (aka the "3 C's").

Using the 3 C's as a top-level framework may well lead you to the correct answer, though it is certainly not the single universally-acknowledged solution to the issue. But what concerned me most about the online case was how the authors argued that the other three options are incorrect for the following reasons:

- The firm's website says: "Growth projection is an outcome of [customer and competitor analysis]; it is not a high-level analysis to use in your framework."
  - □ I would argue that the high-level analyses you choose *should be* the ones that are outcomes of sub-analyses! As a simple example, a profitability analysis is the outcome of revenue and cost analyses.
  - □ Further, a disadvantage with using a category such as "competitor analysis" as a top-level element in your issue tree is that it doesn't focus your attention on answering a specific question. The interviewer could potentially hand you a large document of competitor analyses, but what would you do with it? What is the specific necessary piece of information that you would want to get out of it?
- The firm's website says: "Legal and regulation are not high-level analyses for now – they could be included in a market attractiveness analysis."
  - □ The problem with this reasoning is that the legal barriers are not inherent to the target company or its market: it is only the prospect of a merger that raises them. For example, there is an obvious anti-trust legal barrier that prevents Microsoft and Google from merging, but such an issue would not fit under a market analysis for either company.
- The firm's website says: "Potential synergies can be evaluated only if [the acquirer] already has another company in the same industry. It is an analysis to be applied when relevant."
  - □ My first objection here is that we should include all possible elements of the problem at the outset and then prune off branches if they prove to be irrelevant; we should not ignore them until we determine them to be relevant. As the case introduction did not give us enough information to disregard this element, we should consider it.
  - □ My second objection is that the consulting firm's statement on this issue is simply wrong! You do not need another company in the same industry to create synergies. As we discuss later, firms can create positive synergies by sharing back-office operations over business units in different industries. And negative synergies can be created by companies vertically integrating (such as PepsiCo acquiring Pizza Hut) which are usually in different industries.

Anyway, I choose this example to show that there is plenty of room for a healthy debate. Unfortunately, this case is representative of most cases online; they all create the problem of giving oversimplified answers to complex issues. But if answers were simple and everyone agreed on them, then computers would run businesses, businesses would not need consultants, and there would be no such thing as a case interview...

ABS – "Always Be Structuring" [a]

You should always be thinking of ways to structure the problem or the data that you're working through. Most candidates do this well at the start of the case with a high-level structure, but then they never introduce any other structures into the discussion. Within reason, structure as much as you can. For example, imagine a case interview that, at some point, sounds like this:

Interviewer:	We have decided that we need to offshore some of our labor. What factors should we consider in deciding how to do that?
You:	There's a difference in costs between offshoring and building it here.
Interviewer:	Any other ideas?
You:	Um…. There may be a difference in quality.
Interviewer:	Any other ideas?
You:	Is it possible to offshore the labor? For example, janitors cannot be.
Interviewer:	Any other ideas?
You:	(Silence… panic starts to set in…)

In such a situation, you might get the sense that there's something specific that the interviewer is looking to hear and so you try all combinations to see if you can find it accidentally. But there's probably no specific thing that they're looking for; they're just checking to see how organized your thinking is. Every time they say "any other ideas?" what they're really saying is: "you have no structure". If you ever get to a point in a case where you're searching around for answers, then step back and say something such as:

You:	I feel like I'm randomly brainstorming here. I'd like to back up and put a structure around the question and then try again. I don't know any structures for offshoring, so I'll have to come up with one…

From there, whatever structure you use, how you arrive at it, and whether or not it's completely MECE doesn't matter as much: you've just impressed your interviewer simply by demonstrating that you recognize the importance of structured thinking and, despite a small stumble, are naturally inclined to solve problems in that way. The interviewer, when seeing that you have a structure, will lead you down the right path in your tree to get to what they're looking for.

---

[a] "ABC – Always Be Closing" was the realtors' mantra in David Mamet's wonderfully fast-talking film (and play) *Glengarry Glen Ross*.

How to invent your own structures

Later on, we'll consider a single structure that disaggregates many popular issues that appear in cases. But it's more important to recognize the process by which we can create such frameworks and to be comfortable with disaggregating issues without relying on memorizing pre-existing solutions. Your interviewer doesn't expect (or even want) you to have hundreds of frameworks memorized ahead of time: they want to see how you can break apart a problem that you've never seen before.

In addition, even if you start a case with a well-known framework, you will likely soon encounter a sub-issue of it for which you don't have a framework ready.

Visually, you should write the problem that you're attempting to solve at the top of the paper and then draw lines out from below it to the two to four sub-issues into which you will divide up the problem. Then, looking at each sub-issue in turn, you can build similar trees out from each one until you have a handful of simple problems to solve. By investigating each of these smaller pieces in order, you can easily illuminate the key drivers of the main problem and build a coherent solution.

If you need a minute to think through some possible ideas, then just tell your interviewer that you'd like some time to collect your thoughts. Especially once you're well into a case and are trying to structure a sub-issue that you have encountered, you should always talk aloud through your thought process and the steps that you're taking. Try not to think through problems in silence. At the same time, read your interviewer, especially later in the case. They may be pressed for time and might prefer you to throw some ideas out for discussion rather than to delve into a detailed analysis.

- Put pen to paper quickly. Draw a picture if you're stuck getting started.
  - Imagine that you've reached a point in a case where outsourcing and offshoring labor has become the primary focus. The interviewer asks how you would determine what jobs can be outsourced to an offshore partner.[a] You don't know a structure for that and suddenly your mind goes blank. Start by drawing a picture: not only will it help you visualize some of the key elements, but it will also give you a minute to collect your thoughts.

---

[a] Offshoring is the process of moving jobs to another location, either internally or externally. Outsourcing is the process of moving jobs to an external partner, either locally or internationally. In this example, the client is considering both simultaneously.

▫ Your paper may then look like this:

Exhibit 6-4 An example of one possible problem-solving approach

▫ Goofy? Perhaps, but at least we took a problem that you had no idea how to start on and got started.[a]

- Use your judgment to determine if the interviewer is interested in hearing the details of the thought process you go through in developing your structure or if they are only interested in a more polished explanation at the end.

- Talk through the picture (either in your head or out loud): "let's say we're considering outsourcing the work this person is doing to someone on the other side of this ocean. The most obvious question is: can we physically do that? If their job requires moving physical equipment or meeting with other people, we may not be able to. Or even if the job is solely computer-based, we'd still need a good internet connection to offshore it. We'd still need quality control and feedback measures. Next, how much do we trust this other country we're outsourcing to? We know who's on our side but the other side is a big question mark. Do we trust them to do a good job? Do we trust them with our sensitive data?" These are very elementary thoughts that derive simply from the picture.

  ▫ A good start may be to try to define the issue in the simplest way that you immediately interpret it and then see if there are any components to the issue that don't fit in that definition. For example, to structure ways to grow revenue, you might initially articulate the issue as growing existing revenue streams and then add on that there may be opportunities to grow revenue through new revenue streams.

---

[a] Actually, it may not be that goofy. Leonardo da Vinci and Thomas Edison both used sketches to better understand problems and as starting points in formulating their ideas. Some people have asked me about the value of starting with a sketch and whether it would be considered professional by the interviewer. I believe it's a powerful tool for visualizing different elements of many issues, but you should use whatever method you're comfortable with. I suggest starting with a sketch because it can always helps you get over the "how do I get started?" hurdle when posed with a tough question. Once you have something down on paper, other ideas tend to come more easily.

      □   Trust the first thought that comes to your mind (although you may want to think over it for a second before saying it).

- Finally, take the thoughts you just spoke about and condense them into a structure, such as the example shown in Exhibit 6-5. How you go from a list of ideas to a structure is an art that takes practice, but remember there are many different and equally accurate structures for any given problem.

    □   For example, "to summarize, to determine which jobs or functions to offshore, we'd want to look at three things: the lack of a need for a physical presence and assurances of reliability and security." And indeed, these components do form a good structure for this issue.

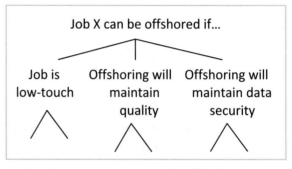

Exhibit 6-5 An example issue tree for offshoring

The offshoring tree example is a little different from the profit tree discussed earlier, as this one disaggregates a qualitative issue instead of a numerical one. It's the same idea, but this tree's entries are statements such that, if all three sub-issues are true, then the top level statement will be true. We sometimes refer to it as an "issue tree" as opposed to just a "logic tree".

Building a tree like this has real value. For example, once you have narrowed part of the issue to checking whether "offshoring would maintain data security", the next obvious steps may include creating an auditing system or signing an agreement to ensure the needed level of security. Such issues were not as obvious before we started the tree.

Another common approach to building such trees is to brainstorm a few items and then see if you can use them as guideposts in creating a structure. For example, if you wanted to put a framework around the different types of variable costs, you might talk through it like this: "I don't know a structure for variable costs, so I'd like to just think through a few things that might be included and see if one comes to mind. Some big ones might be: raw materials, labor, packaging, and shipping. Packaging and shipping are part of the distribution channel. Raw materials are part of procurement and labor is part of manufacturing. So maybe we can divide the costs into those three components: procurement, manufacturing, and distribution." This is certainly not the only structure for variable costs and probably not even the best. But it's effective and the interviewer will appreciate you walking them candidly through your thought process.

If you receive a case where a business has to make a decision, you can almost always use the profit tree. Start by saying something like the first sentence in this chapter and then use the profit tree to determine if the decision will be profitable.

Finally, as a last resort, you can always break something apart into two pieces: "X and not-X". Variable costs could be "manufacturing and non-manufacturing". Culture could be "dress code and non-dress code items". These are not especially enlightening, but at least you know it's completely MECE and it will help you organize your thoughts as you move down one more level.

Some common ways to split a problem in two include: "internal/external", "positives/negatives", or "short-term/long-term". Growth options can be viewed as "organic/inorganic" options. Sales forces can be split into "hunters" (those who go after new customers) and "farmers" (those who maintain and cultivate the existing customer base).

> **However you derive it, the framework you use to solve a problem should give you an immediate insight into that problem. Only employ a framework if it helps to illuminate the real drivers of the issue.**

Once you have outlined your structure and briefly walked the interviewer through it, be confident. Don't ask weak questions such as, "do we have any information on customers?" That sounds like you're shooting around in the dark hoping that you'll hit something. Case interviews are not a game of Battleship. If your structure is sound and you follow it with confidence, then the interviewer will lead you in the right direction. There's limited time in a case so they won't let you search around in the dark if you get off to a good start.

Finally, don't get so caught up in the process of creating a perfect structure that you lose the obvious and creative elements of a particular problem. For example, if you're given a case about a hardware store trying to build out its revenue base, don't attempt to compile a list of every possible new product that they could sell. Doing so may match a previous approach that you memorized and it may be "MECE", but it shows no ability to focus on the key drivers of a problem and to think clearly and creatively within a specific context.

In this example, suggesting that a hardware store grow their revenues by building a membership option on their website to allow customers to trade second-hand building supplies is a much more creative and compelling thought. If you use the Valuation Framework or another approach, it is up to you to add your creativity to the generic drivers (such as "increase number of products" or "increase distribution channels") that's needed to allow the real insights to bloom.

The one framework that will cover at least 80% of your cases

Many books on case interviews give dozens of different structures and frameworks for all the different possible case types that you might encounter in an interview. Does anyone memorize all of them? Often there's no obvious logic to how the author assembled the frameworks and so while you might be able to remember a few of them in the short-term, this method has limited long-term value.

Most of the stress in the interview comes from a lack of confidence in whether you'll remember all of the frameworks correctly. Remember exams in school, when (other) students would try to memorize everything in the few minutes before class started? All that method does is to close your brain to free and creative thought and the things that you "learn" have no lasting value years later.

Memorizing lots of independent solutions in isolation of each other also doesn't allow you to pass the "Why?" test. This could occur where you, as an interviewee, receive a market entry case and proceed to draw out an elaborate two-tiered tree with twenty branches in it that you memorized. The interviewer, impressed with your ability to structure the solution in such detail and so quickly says, "why did you choose this solution? Why did you structure it this way?"... to which, presumably, you would have no good response.

The Valuation Framework in Exhibit 6-6 contains what are likely the ten most common case questions in the form of one integrated and straightforward framework. If you are going to memorize anything, my suggestion is to memorize this. Since there's an obvious logic to it, you'll find that it stays in your mind years later.

While this framework can cover many of the cases that you'll encounter, don't try to force-fit it onto the rest. Case interviews, like all business problems, are never one-size-fits-all issues. I simply present this tree as an alternative to the dozens of separate frameworks given by other resources and to give us a starting point for discussions.

To use the framework in an interview, simply figure out what the objective is and then use the relevant subtree. For example, if the objective of a case is about increasing revenues, ignore anything outside of the revenue subtree. In a Merger and Acquisition (M&A) case, use the M&A tree. If your interviewer guides you to investigate the standalone profitability of the company that we're considering acquiring, then you can build the profit tree out as you progress down that path.

The 10 most popular frameworks are in bold in the chart: Market Entry/New Product and Merger/Acquisition each represent two. Different consulting firms operate in different regions of the tree and thus their cases may be more likely to focus on those regions. Operations-heavy firms, for example, may do more cases based on decreasing costs. Strategic consulting firms consider the entire tree, but many focus on investment decisions, such as valuing a new product introduction or the acquisition of another firm.

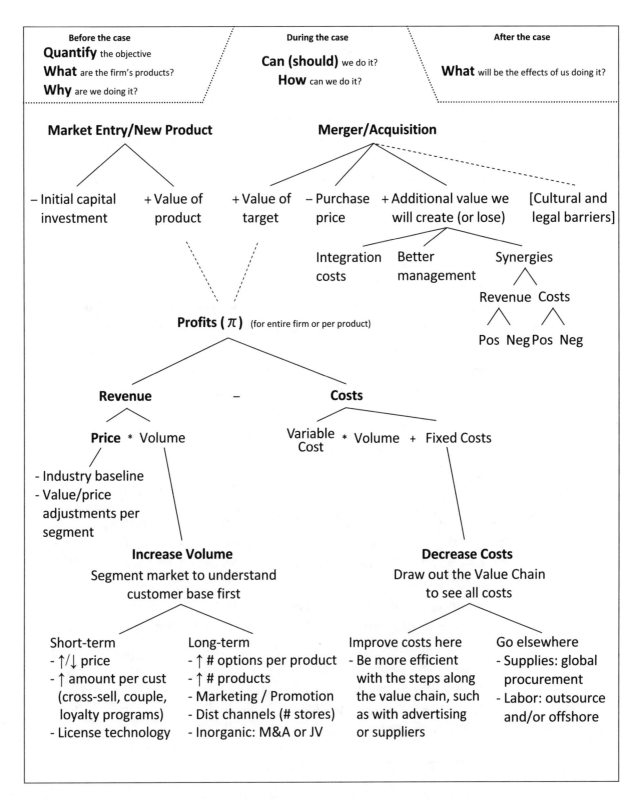

Exhibit 6-6 The Valuation Framework with the 10 most popular case types highlighted

In addition to the Valuation Framework, there are six overarching elements to all cases that appear before, during, and after the core part of the case.

Before the case (clarify these before building your initial structure)

- Quantify the objective or goal of the case.
  - It may seem obvious, but skipping this is one of the most common pitfalls.
- What are our products?
  - We can use the profit tree to represent the financials for an entire company or for each of its product separately. The market share and/or profitability of each product may differ greatly or we may only be interested in one particular product.
- Why do we want to take the proposed action? [Strategy]
  - This is a key simple question to kick off the discussion, even if you only ask it in your own head (and perhaps verify with the interviewer). Usually it should be obvious: to increase profitability or market share, for example. But some acquisitions are defensive, such as to strategically prevent a competitor from making a certain move. Knowing if this is the case early on will help you focus your attention.
  - It may also answer: what will happen if we don't do it?
  - See Appendix 2 for more insight into why this is an important consideration and how it fits into the rest of the approach.

During the case

- Can/should we do it? (Usually most of the case discussion) [Finance]
  - Will the action be profitable for us / will it achieve our objective?
  - Can we afford it? Do we have the resources to perform the action? If not, can we acquire them?
  - Are there legal or cultural barriers?
- How can we do it? (Usually towards the end of the case) [Operations]
  - What's the strategy?
  - What's the implementation plan?
  - How will we finance the needed investment?
  - How will we distribute and advertise the products?
  - Is there a specific lever to pull?

After the case

- What will be the risks and effects of us doing it? [Strategy]
  - What will be the competitors' response?
  - Will we cannibalize our current products?

The case will dictate how much of a role each of the six will play; your interviewer will guide you to the areas that are most important as long as they are convinced that you haven't missed any major points.

What are drivers and levers? Where do customers and competitors fit in?

Drivers are the elements in the organization or situation that are most influential in causing change. For example, revenues and costs are the key drivers of profitability. Legal issues may be a key driver of whether a merger will be successful. Drivers are the moving parts that you have to account for.

Levers are drivers that you can directly control. Revenue is probably not a lever, but advertising can be. Increasing advertising will then increase volume and thus revenue.

Market forces are the external elements in the market that influence your drivers. Customers and competitors are the two key forces that play some role in almost every case and business situation. Customers and competitors can influence the revenue side of a business, but have limited impact on costs. They influence price and volume; they influence what products you produce, where you sell them, and the types of advertising that you do. Customers can influence costs by expressing needs and tastes that drive product design; if companies do not segment and understand their customer base well, they can overdesign and introduce too costly products into the market.

Customers as an entity is neither a driver nor a lever. Imagine asking during a case interview (or an engagement) a weak question such as, "do we have any information on our customers?" The interviewer might turn around and say, "sure, we have lots of information. What do you want to know and why?"

Instead, better targeted questions come from understanding how customers affect each driver in the MECE structure. Examples might be: "is our price competitive with the other products available?" or "has our volume dropped because our products no longer meet our customers' needs?"

1) Profitability, Revenue, and Cost cases

For profitability cases and anything below it on the tree, you may just want to use the relevant part of the Valuation Framework in Exhibit 6-6 as your primary structure. The "During the case" questions are usually implicitly built into those cases. If you want, you can consider adding the "After the case" questions at the end of the case to differentiate yourself from other candidates. It's easy to say we'll outsource labor to reduce costs, but will there be union issues to consider or other risks? And while there may be no direct competitor response to increasing your own profits, if you mention it, it shows that you at least considered it. If you increase your profits by cross-selling a certain product to customers of another product, there may be possible cannibalization; pointing that out will really set you apart from other applicants.

Profitability cases are very common, but sometimes the objective will be hidden at first. Asking "why?" at the start, even if just in your own mind, can help uncover the true profit objective. For example, consider a case such as, "Company X is considering building an oil rig; should they?" or something similar. Ask yourself or your interviewer why they might want to do it. In this situation, the most likely reason is simply that they would do it if it would be profitable. Confirm that suspicion with the interviewer and proceed using the profit tree.

The label "for entire firm or per product" represents a reminder that we can consider profitability for an entire company or for individual products or business units. For example, if a hot dog and hamburger manufacturer is considering expanding its distribution channels, it may be valuable to calculate the profitability (and thus pricing, volume, and costs) for each product separately. Or we may only be interested in one product or business unit in a given case.

Pricing is an interesting subtree that may represent a short discussion in one of these cases, but can also stand on its own as an entire case.

2) Pricing cases

There are probably very few cases that only focus on pricing but questions about how to determine the optimal price for a new or existing product can be a substantial component of a case. Pricing can be one of the most powerful levers that a company can influence to improve its profits.[1] In a case where the interviewer asks you to determine the optimal pricing strategy for a product, first note that we should set prices that maximize our profits. From that starting point, there are many ways that you can attack the issue.

You can use the following pricing system in any pricing component of a case. I suggest considering two levels of granularity when setting and managing prices for a product, as shown below.

1) First, clarify the problem…
   □ For whom are we setting the price? End user or retailers?
   □ Do we have a target profit level?
2) …then set a baseline price…
   □ Start by looking at the industry as a whole. You can calculate a baseline price based the prices of competitor and substitute products. For example, a baseline price for contact lenses could be set so that they would break even with the cost of eyeglasses for the end user.

- You should also calculate a cost-based price as a baseline that we should not fall below.

  - Calculate expected volume, fixed costs (including all R&D costs), and our variable costs. (We should also add our distribution partners' margins to our variable costs if we are setting an end user price and working through a distributor or retailer.) If we have a target profit level, we can consider including that in this price.

  - This will give us our break-even price.

  - Check that any final prices we recommend are at or above the break-even price. If we cannot expect to find a price that does so, we should consider not selling the product at all. (Unless we have significant fixed costs and then we may want to sell it anyway. Even though it would be a net loss, we will at least be earning some of our fixed costs back.)

3) …and finally make price/value adjustments (per market segment)

   - Once we have a baseline, we should adjust it based on how our product compares to our competitors'. You can do this for the market overall (which may be a simplification that case interviews take), but it is most powerful if you segment that market first and then do it for each segment.

     - Are they a hotel chain that serves both vacationers and business travelers? Are they a tire manufacturer that serves both consumer retailers and large trucking companies?

   - The key question to answer is: how do customers perceive our value/price proposition relative to competitors? Based on those analyses, we will set the list price for our products or services. Exhibit 6-7 shows an example of how we can consider the tradeoff between consumer perception of our products' price and benefits relative to our competitors'. The dotted line

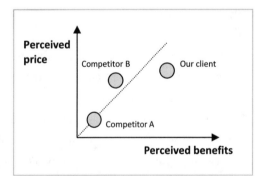

Exhibit 6-7 An example of a consumer perceptions map of product price and benefits

represents the continuum on which consumers expect products to fall. If a new product is introduced at a higher price than the market's existing products, consumers expect that it should offer higher relative benefits.[2]

   - Example questions to answer include: Can we charge a premium for our product within a given segment if it offers unique value? How low can we drop our prices before starting a price war with our main competitors?

If you're introducing a new product or a product that is very different from other options, you can calculate how much added value this product creates and then price it based on that. For example, for a light bulb that uses 50% less electricity, one value estimate is the cost of the electricity saved. The new light bulbs could potentially be priced that much more than other light bulbs, although there may be some difficulty in convincing the customer of the actual value, thus causing the price to be lower.

3) New Product and Market Entry cases

New product and market entry cases are similar case types. The former covers launching a ground-breaking new product; the latter, entering an industry that already has existing players in it. In both cases, the "During the case" questions ("can we do it?" and "how can we do it?") as well as the "After the case" questions ("what will be the risks and effects of doing it?") are especially important and you may want to start the case by clearly articulating that you want to step through each of the three in turn.

In new products and market entry cases, we are considering making an initial capital investment in exchange for expected future profits. The investment is one worth making if the value of those future profits exceeds the cost of the capital by a large enough margin. If we are deciding between three investment options, for example, we'd choose the one that creates the most value by this approach.

See Appendix 2 for the details of how the value of a product derives from the profits that we expect to realize from it. For the purposes of case interviews, though it's enough to simply appreciate that the expected profitability of a product is the key driver of its value.

These types of cases mainly revolve around 2 elements: setting an expected price point and estimating (or determining how to maximize) the volume of the key products that you will sell. You will likely be given the initial capital costs and variable costs per product. You may also be given the expected price; if not, you can use the approach given in the pricing section above. For volume, first calculate the breakeven volume that you do not want to fall below. Then, if we anticipate higher volumes than that, you can calculate the return on investment (ROI). You can wrap up the case with a more qualitative discussion about the forces that can impact your price and volume estimates over time using Porter's 5 Forces.

The key analysis in many new product cases is to calculate the breakeven volume. Given a price, variable costs, and an initial capital investment, how many products do we have to sell in a given time period to breakeven? This is an easy analysis to do. One approach is to write out the equation from the Valuation Framework and solve for volume.

It looks like this:

Value of product = Initial capital investment

Which can be rewritten as:

Price * Volume – [VC * Volume + FC] = Initial capital investment

We can drop the fixed cost (FC) entry from this since we can assume that there are no additional fixed costs beyond the initial capital investment. (In real life, given a multi-year time horizon, we may not be able to make this simplification.) Rewriting the above step gives the standard breakeven volume equation:

Breakeven volume = Initial capital investment / [Price - Variable costs]

You don't need to go through these steps in a case, but there is value in knowing that it's in the tree and you can derive it if needed.

You can also easily derive return on investment from the starting equation: ROI = Value of product (or profits) / Initial capital investment. (You can also ignore the fixed cost entry when working with this equation in a case interview.)

Beyond a breakeven analysis, the case may involve more qualitative discussions about the variables that you should consider when making the introduction. You can note that volume (specifically segmenting the customers to see how we can best sell the product) is probably the most important lever in determining the expected value of the product. You may want to steer straight to it after laying out the structure. Pricing is also important for new product introductions; see the pricing section above for more details on it.

While the profit tree is MECE by itself, a complication with using it for these case types is that it doesn't easily lend itself to isolating the most influential forces in creating or entering a new market. In contrast, in other cases, such as where a company has been losing profits, we can easily use the profit tree to isolate where the problem lies and then, if applicable, back out from it any market forces that may be influencing the change. But in market entry or new product cases, we have to investigate and diagnose all of these possible causes of potential future issues without having the benefit of seeing the symptoms. Porter's 5 Forces gives us a systematic method to consider all of these forces that may affect the entire industry.

Articulate that the profit tree is your central framework, but that you will use the 5 Forces as a

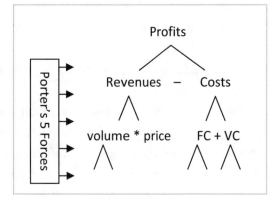

Exhibit 6-8 Porter's 5 Forces helps us the model all of the external forces that influence the drivers of profitability

way to structure the most significant external influences that could affect the various drivers and subdrivers in your profit tree, as shown in Exhibit 6-8.

Porter's 5 Forces are:

- Intensity of competitors
- Bargaining power of buyers
- Threat of new entrants   these four can affect your revenue
- Threat of substitutes
- Bargaining power of suppliers   this one can affect your costs

The industry's barriers to entry determine the degree of the threat of new entrants, some of which are cost-based (capital requirements, access to distribution channels, learning curve…) and some of which are revenue-based (high switching costs, product identity and differentiation needs, expectation of retaliation…).

> **Porter's 5 Forces can help you structure all of the possible external changes that may affect future values for price, volume, and costs in the profit tree.**

Highlight each of the five explicitly and discuss – or ask – how each of these forces could allow you to create sustainable advantage or how they could pose future risks. For example, if there are a limited number of suppliers, could that limit your ability to grow volume in the future?

There are some differences between the market entry and new product introduction case types. With a new product introduction case, your focus will be on determining whether the product matches customer needs (by segmenting the market), pricing, and whether it will be profitable. You can then use the 5 Forces to analyze future risk: "could competitors move in?", for example. For a market entry case, there may be less emphasis on product design, pricing, and profitability, and more emphasis on investigating each of the 5 Forces as they currently exist in the market.

Once you have this as a starting point, the implementation plan should follow naturally in the conversation.

Sometimes, instead of a case where your client is thinking of entering a new market (or merging or adding a new product), they will have already taken action then discovered it isn't working and they want you to find out why it's failing. The same approach will work. For example, if a market entry is failing, look at all of the 5 Forces to see if any are turning out to be more problematic than the client anticipated.

Finally, when in the last part of the case, consider the effects the action. The threat of cannibalizing your own products may be a key part of the case or it may simply be one sentence that you can add on at the end to show your interviewer that you've got a good sense of how all the machinery works together.

4) Mergers and Acquisition cases (M&A)

M&A may be one of the most complex case type but you won't have to drill down very deeply into each of the sub trees in such a case.

The approach given here is primarily from an acquisition perspective because there are rarely true "mergers of equals". When the term merger is used, there is usually one company that is larger than the other or one that is clearly taking the lead. Therefore we can approach such cases as if they are acquisitions with the only real difference being that, in a merger, the two companies will likely exchange shares as part of the deal and the resulting leadership team will be a mix of both firms' leaders.

The two main things that you want to know for the "During the case" questions ("can we do it?" and "how can we do it?"), as detailed in the Valuation Framework, are:

- Will we create significant value by making the acquisition?
  - Value created = Standalone value of the target - purchase price + the additional value we can add through synergies or similar
- Will the government legally allow us to proceed? Is there a good cultural fit?
  - The main legal issue is anti-trust legislation
  - For two companies to work together effectively towards a common goal, they have to share similar behavioral norms and comparable cultures

The value created by an acquisition = the value of the target *minus* the price we pay for it *plus* any additional value we can add to it. More concisely, does the value that we expect to create through synergies or better management significantly exceed the premium that we'll likely have to pay to acquire the target?

Appendix 2 has more details on exactly what we mean by the "value of the target" and how it is impacted by the target's profits. For the purposes of the case interview, though, it is likely enough just to know that there is an independent value of the firm that we are considering acquiring and its value is largely based on expected future profitability.

While case interviews are unlikely to get into the details of valuation, taking a valuation perspective helps us to move directly to the key issues. For example, the interviewer may ask you what some of the main drivers of the target's standalone value are. In the tree, it's easy to see that they are price, volume, and costs – all of which are influenced in turn by customer preferences and competitive pressures.

It is interesting to note that acquirers typically pay about 30% more for a target's equity than its valuation is worth[3] (and thus an acquirer's stock price drops an average of 1-3%

after the announcement of the acquisition). The reason is that if an acquirer is expected to add 30% additional value through synergies or better management, the shareholders of the target who do not sell their shares for sale as part of the acquisition will see the value of their holdings increase by that 30% value. Therefore acquirers have to pay a 30% premium to convince a majority of shareholders to tender their shares for either cash or shares in the acquirer. Such a step is necessary to gain control of the target and allow the deal to be completed.

Given this, the basic question that most acquisitions reduce to is: is the net value of the synergies we can create significantly greater than the premium we are going to have to pay to acquire the firm? If yes, then the acquisition is likely a good deal. If not (which is most often the case[4]), then the deal is probably not the best investment for our resources.

Synergies are perhaps the most interesting aspect of M&A cases. Synergies can be positive or negative and can occur in any of the drivers under the profit tree, but they are especially prevalent in volume and fixed costs.

Positive revenue synergies might include cross-selling opportunities or cases where you can reach a broader customer base by offering a complete solution instead of just individual components.

Negative revenue synergies can occur when you change the branding of the acquired company to your own brand and then see a decrease in net volume. This happens when you try to increase market share in an area where you have already saturated the market. For example, assume that 1 out of 3 people in a city drink your brand of coffee. If you are already serving them with your current stores, then acquiring a competitor to increase your number of stores in that city will not change your current volume; you'll simply lose the volume that your competitor was serving previously and thus see a net decrease.

A negative revenue synergy can also occur when customers prefer to maintain a minimum of two suppliers. If such customers previously used both the acquirer and the target as their two suppliers, they may prefer to move half of their orders to a third party after the merger. Horizontal integration can thus create negative revenue synergies because the industry decreases its diversity.

PepsiCo encountered another interesting negative revenue synergy after it acquired Pizza Hut and Taco Bell restaurants in the late 1970s. By doing so, PepsiCo as a corporation instantly became competitors to some of their previous customers (such as Domino's Pizza) and many of those then switched to only serving Coca-Cola. Vertical integration can thus create negative revenue synergies because a firm will likely increase its number of possible rivals.

Positive cost synergies might include combining functional units such as finance, marketing, procurement, and operations. It also gives the combined organization increased buying power from its suppliers and potentially lowers the advertising need if you acquired a major competitor.

Negative cost synergies typically occur when the newly merged companies needs a new management layer to communicate across its entities. We can also consider this the cost of implementing the acquisition.

After answering the "During the case" questions ("can we do it?" and "how can we do it?"), you can move on to the "After the case" questions ("what will be the risks and effects of doing it?").

5) Volume

Quantitatively, volume = market size * market share. Volume is a critical subcomponent of every case type shown in the Valuation Framework and it is almost always a key driver in growing revenue and profits or introducing a new product.

> **Volume is the element that best represents customers and competitors. If applicable, move to it quickly and suggest segmenting the market to determine whether your products are meeting your customers' needs.**

Market size is the total volume of a product (such as all brands of bleach) purchased by a defined market segment during a defined period of time.[a] A market segment might be the entire US population or it might be high-income households in the southwest, as an example. Market size may have some organic growth, but it's typically not a lever you can pull.

Market share, on the other hand, is typically more dynamic. Your market share and the market share of your competitors is a critical data point for starting a discussion about how your company is faring in the market. It gives you insight into how well your products are fulfilling the needs of the customers relative to your competitors.

There are many levers and drivers that affect volume and almost all of them affect market share. So how do you know which lever to pull and to what extent? A good start is to segment the customers. You could start by saying something like: "I would like to segment the market and look at the value drivers for each customer segment. Then, once we understand who our customers are and what's important to them, I would look at our products and see which segments we're providing value to and which we're simply not representing. Once we have a sense of this landscape, there are many levers we can pull."

---

[a] Market size can also be the total revenue or spend in the market. That version can be more valuable when sizing a market for a new product entry or a private equity deal because in those cases we are ultimately only concerned with how much money is out there and how much of it we can expect to get.

Segmenting customers is a great start but it may not be relevant to every case; read your interviewer to see how far you should push there. There are many ways to segment the market. The three main overall categories are:

Increasing complexity and insights

- *A Priori*: **Who** are our potential customers?
  - Demographic: age, family size, gender, occupation, income, …
  - Geographic: country, region, state, zip, urban/rural, …
  - Psychographic: active, family-oriented, conservative, …
- Behavioral: **How, when, and where** are they purchasing?
  - Different segments might include consumers who are casual users, repeat users, heavy users, …
  - Or they may include consumers who purchase online, at bars, or in the supermarket, for example. Consumers can use the same product at different times for different reasons.
- Needs-based: **Why** are they acting the way they do?
  - The attributes in this category can differ greatly.
  - Example segments may include consumers who…
    - View themselves as style leaders or product connoisseurs and make purchases accordingly.
    - Make purchases based on long-term connections to a brand.
    - Make purchases based on product comfort, safety, price, delivery experience, or the product's relevance in building their social status.

The most insightful customer segmentations often use a combination of categories.

After segmenting the market, the next step is to determine the commonalities across all of the segments in terms product attributes, marketing, and/or distribution. Much of what you offer the market will remain constant across all segments. For example, while Coca-Cola markets and distributes their products in many different ways for multiple segments, their core product remains constant across each. Then you can isolate the small set of most influential number of options that differentiate each segment.

There is no universal substructure for volume so you should use whatever you're most comfortable with and whatever makes the most sense to you. Three different methods of structuring ways to increase volume on the demand-side follow. Each has different strengths and so perhaps knowing all three and when to use them would be most useful. Note that the sub-elements of the first two are basically the same; simply the top-level organization of them differs.

Three ways to structure sales volume:

The 4 P's: Diagnosing the different <u>drivers</u> of our current (low) volume

- Price
  - Product is not priced competitively
- Product
  - Product doesn't reflect customer needs
    - Note that this could be the case for all of our competitors as well, thus causing a decrease in the total market size
  - We don't have enough products or enough options per product
- Placement
  - We don't have the right quantity or quality of distribution channels
  - We aren't cross-selling or bundling enough
  - Our sales team isn't the right size or lacks the correct focus
- Promotion
  - We don't have the right quantity or quality of advertising

---

"Short-term / long-term": Structuring all of the <u>levers</u> available to increase volume

- **Short-term:** levers that you can pull without changing costs
  - Increase/decrease price (in rare cases when price elasticity is negative, increasing price will increase volume)
  - Increase amount sold per customer
    - For example: cross-sell, couple products together (bundle), or create loyalty programs
  - License technology (provides another revenue stream)
- **Long-term:** levers that may require a new annual budget cycle
  - Increase the number of options per product
    - For example: sell 21 flavors of ice cream instead of 5 or sell multiple product sizes
  - Increase the number of products or change existing products to better reflect customer needs
  - Increase or change marketing / promotion
  - Changing packaging, advertising, or sales force strategies
  - Increase the number of distribution channels
    - For example: increase number of stores or sell over the internet
  - Inorganic growth: Acquisition / Merger / Joint Venture

Mathematical approach: Structuring <u>numbers</u>

- Volume = Market size x Market share

6) Fixed and variable costs

As with volume, there are no "official" substructures for fixed costs or variable costs partly because determining what counts as a fixed versus a variable cost in most organizations is very complicated. Typically 40% of labor is considered fixed and 60% variable, for example. In a case interview, you will likely not need to differentiate between fixed and variable costs.

Drawing out the value chain and/or using the cost substructure suggested in the Valuation Framework may be a good starting point; actual details may depend on the direction that the case is heading in. A value chain describes all of the steps in a manufacturing process that add value (and incur costs). Exhibit 6-9 has one example.

Purchasing / Raw materials
Machine usage
Labor / Assembly
Packaging
Distribution
Advertising and Sales
Customer Service
(+Corporate overhead, R&D, ...)

Exhibit 6-9 An example value chain

The value chain lets you follow the product's creation from raw materials to a finished product on a store shelf. It's a good structure because it allows you to visualize where the entries are coming from and it's hard to miss something. If you write out the value chain thinking about the Tickle-Me-Elmo toy moving from fabric to the end user, following the steps along the way, you probably won't miss any major elements. We can add customer support costs at the end of the value chain if appropriate.

Another possible structure for fixed costs is an invention of mine, the "3 P's": People, Places, and Processes. It covers the main elements of fixed costs. Some labor ("People") is fixed; Plant, Property, and Equipment ("Places") is fixed; and then there's lighting, technology, and other corporate overhead, such as SG&A ("Processes").

The Valuation Framework is not only easy to remember; it reflects how CEOs think about their companies and their possible actions and options

Each one of the ten frameworks in the Valuation Framework in Exhibit 6-6 is MECE and in total they should provide a good frame of reference for many of your cases. There are many ways to structure each of the case types and where you focus your attention will depend on the case – your interviewer will guide you down a certain path after they're convinced that you have laid out a good structure.

One key take-away from the Framework is that growing volume is arguably a sub-component of most cases; similarly, growing revenue and cutting costs might also be key drivers for many cases. You will likely not dive down more than two to three levels in any given case, but knowing that you could drill down a few more levels in an M&A case, for example, should give you confidence.

Personally, I found the short- and long-term structure to increase volume a very helpful tool during case interviews; especially since volume is a lever to pull in many cases.

How to use the Valuation Framework in a case

1) Start a case by articulating the objective in one word if possible. Is the objective "profits", "revenue", "costs", "merger", "new product", or "market entry"?

   ▫ The interviewer should give you this in the introduction to the case, but it's up to you to figure out which key drivers or levers the case focuses on. Figure it out and write it down at the top of your paper and build your tree down from it. This sounds simple, but if you miss this step, it will be tough to recover effectively.

   ▫ Profitability is such a common case type that you may even want to ask yourself, "would the profitability structure be best here?" (Or, at least, "is profitability a subcomponent of this case?").

2) Ask a clarifying question or two, such as: what are the company's products or services?

   ▫ If there is a list of specific products, write them toward the bottom of your paper along the right side of the vertical line. Leave room to the right and along the top of the product list to build a table if data becomes available later about the products, such as market share, margins, level of competitive advantage, or growth rates. Similarly structure the competitors' names in a table if they are mentioned.

3) Once you have your objective, draw the tree underneath it, even just to the first level.

   ▫ You can ask the interviewer for a minute to think it over and write out your structure. If you know exactly what structure you're using, though, you may want to talk through it as you write it out.

4) Start with the top level: "let's disaggregate profits into revenue and costs." Then move one level down and talk through the entire level before diving deeper into a specific area: "the components of revenue are price and volume; under costs we have fixed costs and variable costs."

   ▫ Look to the interviewer for guidance on where to focus and develop the substructures as you dive down into them. Don't dive down too far into one branch until you have discussed all of the other branches on the same level – this is very important! In other words, don't go from profits to revenue to price without explaining that you have costs and a number of other sub-branches to investigate. If you find yourself diving too deeply in one area, step back and let the interviewer know that you haven't lost sight of the big picture: that there are a number of other areas you still need to investigate.

The last step in a case interview: the "Summary for the CEO"

At the end of the case, the interviewer may ask you to summarize everything that you've learned for the CEO. You have about thirty seconds; imagine you just ran into the CEO in the elevator.

- I'd recommend not asking for a minute to collect your thoughts here.
  - If you imagine the CEO/elevator scenario, it should be clear why you need to be able to immediately summarize you work and findings at any time without hesitation.
- Start by reiterating the objective from the top of the case in one sentence.
  - For example: "you asked us to investigate ways to increase profits by $50 million over the next three years." If you underline or circle the objective at the start of the case, you'll be able to find it immediately.
- Then immediately give the specific answer or solution that you are recommending. Don't hedge your answers; make a recommendation and be confident in it. If you're unsure that it's a perfect solution, say it and then add to it the risks and other areas for investigation.
  - For example: "we recommend forming a joint venture with Company X and building a full product solution that you can offer to your core customer base. Doing so has a few risks, though, and so we plan to isolate and quantify them in more detail."
- Follow this with the 2 or 3 key reasons why you are suggesting the given solution. To do this, you can go to your tree and talk through the options and the path you choose: "we looked into the sub-drivers of profitability A, B, and C and decided that X was the best option."
- Finally, you can end with something such as: "we believe we can achieve this goal in three years but still need to check that all of the data supports it; we'll keep working and get back to you in a few weeks."

General advice

What about other structures, such as the 3 C's or the BCG Matrix?

Kenichi Ohmae, a famous business strategist, former McKinsey consultant, and author of *The Mind of the Strategist*, coined the term "3 C's" (Customer, Competitor, and Company), which he refers to as the strategic triangle. He writes: "A successful strategy is one that ensures a better or stronger matching of corporate strengths to customer needs than is provided by competitors."[5] The 3 C's framework highlights the key stakeholders in a business strategy, but as a structure, it has limited use in case interviews. It does not provide a MECE framework to disaggregate any particular objective.

The 3 C's has customers in it but not suppliers; it has competitors but no other market pressures. Customers and competitors are key market forces to consider, but bring them into your analysis as they affect certain elements of your tree, such as volume, pricing, and the key aspects of your product.

If you need to consider customers and competitors directly, a better replacement might be to look at two separate structures: the value chain and the 5 Forces. The value chain follows costs (or value creation) from suppliers to the end customer; the 5 Forces model all external market pressures. The value chain structures all of the elements inside a company; the 5 Forces, all of the forces outside of it.

The BCG Matrix is another framework often suggested for use in case interviews. It is a 2x2 matrix plotting Market Growth Rate against Relative Market Share. It labels products with high market share as either "Cash Cows" or "Stars" and suggests that they generate the cash that fosters the growth of less mature products. This assumes that high market share always generates high cash flow, but there are numerous obvious exceptions to this assumption. A firm that is temporarily selling a product at a loss or very slim margin may likely have a high market share but the product obviously won't generate a significant positive cash flow.

Market share can also be tricky to quantify: the market share of Oster's toaster oven could change based on if the market is defined as all toaster ovens, all toaster-type products, or all cooking and heating products. Jack Welch discovered that his "be #1 or #2, or close, fix, or sell it" mantra for GE's products pressured his employees to very narrowly define the market that they were competing in so that they were always #1 or #2 in terms of share. Only by redefining the markets more broadly did innovative growth opportunities arise.[6]

While the BCG Matrix can be a useful starting point to visually organize multiple products in a firm's portfolio, I don't present it here because I don't think that you need it. If you receive a long list of products in a case, I would first start by collecting the data in a table. Then if you think it would be useful, you can easily sketch a quick graph that displays the data using market share, growth rate, profitability, or any other characteristics along the axes as is relevant for the data you have and the objective of your case.

There are many other models that I don't mention for the same reason: you don't need them to solve any particular case interview problem and they're easy enough to invent on your own. Another interesting one worth at least mentioning, though, is the McKinsey/GE 9-box Matrix that was a direct response to the BCG Matrix. While it avoids the pitfalls of the BCG Matrix, it is still a simplistic approach to visualizing corporate strategic positions. The matrix plots "industry attractiveness" (external forces) against "core competencies" (internal forces). These are the two contrasting characteristics at the center of the economists' debate over which most drive corporate performance. I propose instead that the approach discussed earlier of using Porter's 5 Forces to evaluate external forces and the value chain to evaluate internal ones is more powerful and insightful.

Structure quantitative data and talk through your math out loud

As mentioned earlier, use a table to capture collections of data points, such as the names of products and their market share, growth rates, and profit margins. Tables or similar visual representations can be very valuable for capturing other values as well.

When doing a math problem, write out all zeroes and talk through the steps you're taking. If the interviewer gives you a few values and then you're silent for thirty seconds before presenting them with a final answer, they can't help you out if it's wrong.

Start by saying what you're trying to calculate: "we know the profit level we need to reach; I want to calculate how many new customers we'll need". Then write out the values you'll use to make the calculation. Talk through each step as you work through it. If you get an intermediate value wrong, the interviewer will step in to help you if they know what you're up to; otherwise, they can't.

On paper, to divide 50 million by 200, write the values out (without commas initially if you have values ending in zeroes; it's easier to add the commas in later):

    50000000 / 200

And then cross out the zeroes and add the commas to the resulting values:

    500,000 00 / 2 00 = 250,000

If you receive more complicated values, such as "50,125 / 212", round both values to get: 50,000/200, then use the above method to get a ballpark figure (250). Then ask if that's okay or whether you should do the full math. If you have to get a more accurate value, no need to worry about the decimal place: as soon as you see 236 come out of the long division, you know you're finished with the calculation since it's close to the approximation.

Some math problems may require you to approximate values and make assumptions. The only number you really need to know going into an interview is that there are about 300 million people in the United States. From that value, you can derive just about any estimate you may need to make. To approximate the total US market size of greeting cards, for example, you might simply say, "I receive about 15 cards in December and maybe 8 the rest of the year; assume that's average for all 300 million people in the US and the market size is about 7 billion."

Another good math trick to know is the Rule of 72. If you want to estimate how many years it takes for revenue or profits to double if they are growing at a certain annual rate, just divide 72 by that rate. For example, profits growing at 8% annually will double in about 9 years; profits growing at 6% annually will double in about 12 years. (This estimate is accurate within about 1% of the actual value.)

How to "talk like a consultant"

If you have any friends or mentors who have been consultants, try to practice cases with them. Even give them a case and see how they approach it. If you don't have that opportunity, the sample dialogue here should give you a good starting point.

Talking like a consultant does not mean using a lot of buzzwords. In fact, with a few exceptions, it means the opposite. Consultants communicate effectively by using the same method we just used in working through cases: they organize their thoughts into a tree and then move down the tree in an orderly path. Former McKinsey consultant Barbara Minto articulated this idea in her book, *The Minto Pyramid Principle*. The key idea is to take all of the thoughts you want to convey and group them into two to four sets such that all of the elements in each set support the same general argument or thought. Those two to four general arguments together support your overall governing thought or the thesis of your communication. Then you can repeat this with each of the smaller sets and so on, if you like.

The reason that this is so valuable is that it immediately puts a framework and storyline around the conversation.

Using buzzwords can be valuable of doing so helps to articulate your thoughts more concisely. It's easier to use the phrase "customer loyalty" than to spend two minutes explaining the concept behind it. But if you're not very familiar with such terms, don't worry about trying to learn them.

Finally, be concise. Don't ever talk for more than about a minute without giving the interviewer time to respond or point you in the right direction. When people get nervous, they tend to talk more, so practice doing cases with tough interviewers. Try doing a couple of mock interviews in a suit; a small change such as that can make you feel less comfortable the first time you try it. And don't keep talking for too long even if the interviewer is nodding their head as if in complete interest and agreement.

> **Synthesize. Don't just repeat the facts that the interviewer gives you; figure out what they mean and then share your insights.**
>
> **One way to synthesize is to ask yourself, "How will my future actions be affected by the information I've just collected? What will I do (or not do) now that will be different than before?"**

Being able to summarize your entire approach with one sentence is a nicety that consultants continuously aim for in their communications and so it's also a valiant goal for you in your interviews. Consider a case where the client asked us if we should develop a new product X. You've taken a minute to collect your notes and now you want to communicate your overall approach and set the dialogue in motion. Compare these two possibilities:

1) "Creating value is our primary business objective and so therefore we should introduce this new product only if the value we expect to create from it exceeds the initial investment cost – and it exceeds it significantly enough to justify the cost of that capital." [Summary of the Valuation Framework in Exhibit 6-6.]
   - From that starting point, you could elaborate at the next level of detail in the structure: "On the first branch of the tree, expected value created is the net present value of all future profits which we can derive by modeling expected revenue and costs streams. To estimate these, in turn, we'd need to determine expected pricing, sales volume, fixed and variable costs. Customer segmentation, competitor reactions, and other external forces would all impact that model. On the second branch of the tree, we would need to estimate the initial capital cost required to start selling the first product."

2) "I'd like to look at the product itself, its advantages and disadvantages, and now it compares to the other products in the market. Then I'd look at our customers, their value drivers, and the distribution options to reach them. Then I'd look at the competitive landscape and the possible competitive reactions. Finally, I'd look at the funding options and the cost of any debt we'd take on to finance the project." [A variation on the 3 C's, with costs added.]

Both options are fundamentally correct and a candidate using either could well go on to crack the case, impress the interviewer, and get the job. But the first option gets right to the point with specific next steps that no one can get lost after hearing it in terms of the overall direction that you're planning to take.

Top 5 mistakes that interviewees make

1) They don't clarify and quantify the objective as the very first step in the case.

2) They don't start attacking the problem with a structure or they use a structure that doesn't help to illuminate the drivers of the case's objective.

   □ Before you build your structure, make sure you articulate your assumptions and allow the interviewer to verify or question them. For example, if you receive a case about rolling out a new product, perhaps your first thought is to layout the rollout timeline as your central structure. Explain this to the interviewer before you do it; perhaps what they want you to question whether the rollout should even occur!

3) They create a good structure, but they don't explain it concisely to the interviewer at the start. Practice walking through the key elements of your framework for attacking the problem in 30 seconds. Don't go into any detail about each element – just give the interviewer a sense of the overall landscape. Then read the interviewer for direction about whether you should explain certain elements in more detail.

4) They create and share their structure early on but they don't follow it. If your structure has revenues and costs as the top two drivers, start diving down into them: don't mention those are your top drivers and then ask about competitors. Stick to your structure and have confidence in it. If it's MECE, all of the important elements in the case will come out somehow from it.

5) They start off with a good structure and follow it for a while, but then they lose their structured thinking. At any time in the case, when you are asked a question, such as: "what are some of the risks of doing X?" go back to your original structure and see if you can leverage it to answer the question. If not, consider suggesting a new structure to answer the question.

   □ The summary to the CEO should be a structured recap of the entire case conversation in 30-60 seconds.

Final thoughts

No one is perfect. You'll make a few mistakes in every interview and case you try. Even your interviewers made mistakes when they were interviewing. Be calm and move on if you trip up. No one's perfect and you don't want to let one little error derail the rest of your interview. If you feel like you're off course, take a few seconds to relax. Be honest with your interviewer that you need a second to get your thoughts back on track.

Ask for help if you need it. The interviewer wants you to do well.

> **Imagine the interviewer is a team member who's there to support you. After talking through how you plan to structure the case, ask for their advice. Ask if you're heading in the right direction.**

Practice, practice, practice. Only by doing cases in an interview-like setting will you become confident with them.

Hopefully you will find the Valuation Framework useful as you begin to form your own approach to case interviews and thinking about disaggregating business issues. It's surprising to me how often I see fundamental concepts, such as ways to increase volume, disaggregated in non-MECE and unintuitive ways even in professional publications. Having said that, don't worry about being 100% MECE in a framework you use in an interview; as much as possible, though, try to keep your frameworks intuitive. Show the interviewer where they came from and the line of reasoning that you are using. Simple and intuitive frameworks are *much* more likely to be MECE than complicated ones.

Be flexible. You may prefer to approach a case on outsourcing by looking at the value chain for opportunities while your interviewer prefers starting with an organizational chart. It doesn't mean that your way is wrong; you simply have to be open to switching frameworks depending on the data and the coaching that your interviewer gives you.

Interviews are not tests. They're a meeting where you're both deciding if you would make a good team working together. You can decide that you wouldn't want to accept the job after the interview if the fit isn't right for you.

7 *Sample case interview dialogue*

Three sample dialogues are included below. They are based on actual cases and discussions, but have been cleaned and abridged to highlight the key components. They are not meant to represent a perfect interaction between the interviewer and candidate, but they should a sense of a good conversational dynamic.

Sample dialogue #1: Determining the cause of a profit decline

Interviewer: Our client is a manufacturer of exercise equipment. They have been gaining market share over the last couple of years but have experienced declining profits. Why? What should they do?

You: *[Your thought process: summarize case, verify specific objective, and get a sense what the client's products are (the "before the case" steps from Exhibit 6-6) – these will inform your structure.]*

OK, so our objective is to increase profits while hopefully maintaining our strong market share position. Does the client have a particular target, for example, such as to see a 5% profit increase over the next 12 months?

Interviewer: They did not, but that sounds like the right goal.

You: Before we get started, can you give me a quick overview of the client's products?

Interviewer: The make exercise bikes, treadmills, elliptical machines, those types of things.

You: Great. Can you give me a minute or two to collect my thoughts?

Interviewer: Please do. *[Interviewer starts checking her Blackberry.]*

You: *[You spend about a minute drawing out the main components of a profit tree, similar to the one in Exhibit 6-6.]*

OK, here's how I would like to approach this issue. *[Interviewer puts away her Blackberry and gives you her full attention.]* I'd like to investigate the drivers of our profitability at the top level by looking at revenues and costs. I would propose doing this for the company as a whole first and then if relevant, we can do it for individual products as a deeper dive later. On the revenue side, I'd like to know what changes they've seen in price and volume. On the costs side, I'd like to know how their variable costs have changed.

Interviewer: Do you need to know the changes in volume? I already mentioned that their market share has increased recently.

You:	*[This is a small stumble, but you don't let it affect your confidence. Everyone makes mistakes! Actually, since volume=market size*market share, knowing that market share has increased does not necessarily mean that volume has increased, since the market size could have grown…]*
	Um… right, I forgot you mentioned it. I assume the total market size has not changed dramatically?
Interviewer:	No.
You:	OK, then we can assume our volume has increased. How about price and variable costs?
Interviewer:	Prices have dropped and costs are going up.
You:	Both of those would cause a drop in profits. Pricing can be one of the most powerful levers a company can control, so let's start there. How do we currently price our products?
Interviewer:	We match the lowest price in the market.
You:	So some of our competitors have been dropping their prices and we are following their lead…
Interviewer:	Right.
You:	*[Pricing should be set to maximize profits for the client. You can base your prices off of the amount of value that you bring to your customers. One such approach is detailed in Chapter 6, which you follow here…]*
	Perhaps we should consider a new pricing strategy. I like to think about pricing this way: First we want to have some sense of where prices are moving in the industry, for example, as influenced by new competitors or substitutes. Then, with that as a baseline, we should segment the market and determine the value drivers of the consumers in each segment, for example… *[You draw out a quick chart similar to the one in Exhibit 6-7.]* As the chart shows, consumers balance perceived benefits against perceived prices, so we should only be matching the lowest-priced competitor in a market segment if we have similar perceived benefits as they do. Additionally, we should be wary of consistently following their price drops because that could spark a price war from which no one will benefit.
Interviewer:	Good points. It turns out that the client has not segmented the market and is simply following the lowest-priced competitor in the industry.
You:	That sounds like something we should change.
	[We move to the second main step in the pricing approach you outlined above…]
	Let's do a quick segmentation now then. I imagine there are two key segments in this industry: membership-driven fitness centers and home gyms. Each segment will have different needs. Commercial

gyms will value robust equipment that will last for hundreds of thousands of miles of use with little maintenance. Home gyms will value cheaper products that are good enough for one or two people to use.

Interviewer: Right. The client builds robust commercial-grade equipment with great after-sale service support but they sell them through consumer-facing retailers. They have to keep their prices low in those channels to maintain their market share.

You: Then they should stop selling through those channels and sell directly to commercial gyms. They should raise their prices to match their position on the price/benefit map in that market segment.

Interviewer: Good. Anything else?

You: I think that's it...

Interviewer: We mentioned variable costs were increasing earlier...

You: *[Now you're just being careless. If you write down your initial structure for approaching the problem at the start of the case and always have it in front of you, you should easily be able to see where you are in the overall picture.]*

Right, I forgot.

Interviewer: The main increases in variable costs have been due to the client building service centers for repairing their equipment.

You: We should determine the cost of doing that and check whether the perceived value of it to commercial consumers justifies a high enough price point to cover those costs. My guess is that gyms prefer to have maintenance workers come to their location because they have hundreds of pieces of equipment there that can be serviced together.

Interviewer: Good thoughts. OK, you just met the CEO in the elevator, what do we tell him?

You: *[1 sentence summary of objective; 1 sentence summary of solution; a few sentences giving the main reasons why you're proposing the solution.]*

We've been investigating causes of your recent profit declines. We believe we can increase our profits by selling to commercial gyms instead of to consumers through retailers. Such a customer class is a better match for the qualities of our products. We also believe the recent investment in service centers may not be worth the expense especially if you focus on this segment and want to do a more detailed benefit/cost analysis. We'll get back to you in a few weeks with the full results.

Interviewer: Sounds good.

Feedback

This was a quick case and you drove to the key solutions quickly. Good setup, good structure, and a good closing for the case. A few areas to improve on for next time:

- After building out your initial structure (in this case, profits = price * volume - costs), go back to the data that you've collected already and see if you can plug some of it in. Doing so would have helped avoid the small initial stumble, although you recovered from it very strongly.

- Another key area to improve on here is to reference the main structure throughout the case. After spending a few minutes on the revenue side, it's probably a good idea to at least mention that you've been diving deep into half of the structure and that the other half – costs – should be investigated.

- Finally, to really differentiate yourself, build out the conversation a bit with some more creative suggestions and perhaps relevant analogies from your own experiences. Getting to the answer quickly can help you gain confidence and may impress the interviewer, but doing so doesn't always give you many options to really show off your creative thinking!

Sample dialogue #2: Determining how to react to a competitive threat

Interviewer:	Your client is a manufacturer of keypads for wireless phones. They have a strong market position – about 60% of all cell phones sold in the world use their keypads. The CEO recently heard that another company has built a hologram-style device that can project a full screen keyboard onto flat surfaces and does not require any physical space on the cell phone itself. He is worried and has asked you what it will mean to his business and what he can do about it.
You:	*[Your thought process: summarize case, verify specific objective, and get a sense what the client's products are – these will inform your structure.]*
	To be clear, our client is the CEO of a cell phone keypad manufacturing company and he wants to know if and how to react to a possible substitute product in his industry.
Interviewer:	Correct.
You:	Are there any specific objectives?
Interviewer:	No, that's all the information we have.
You:	OK, can I have a moment to collect my thoughts?
Interviewer:	Yes.
You:	*[The CEO is worried how a new product will impact his sales. First we want to get some sense of what this product will do in the market and then we can determine if and how to react. A good way to model the first item*

would be to consider the value chain of the competitor, which is what you sketch out on paper, such as the one in Exhibit 7-1 below.] Here's how I would approach this problem. Let's consider the value chain of the competitor to get a sense of what the product's hurdles are to threatening our market position. Then, if we determine there is a viable threat, we can consider strategic reactions.

Interviewer: Sounds good.

You: Following the value chain down, we might want to develop some insight into the costs of producing this device... does it require expensive materials or sophisticated labor? We should determine how strong their relationships are with the cell phone manufacturers.

> Purchasing / Raw materials
> Machines
> Labor / Assembly
> Packaging
> Distribution (to cell phone OEMs)
> Advertising

Exhibit 7-1 A value chain for the hologram keypad

Will they be able to build the capacity the OEMs require? Can they gain their trust that they can depend on them enough to develop a new product around this device that currently only has one possible supplier? Finally, there's the customer element – consumer demand is what ultimately sets the value chain in motion. Do customers want this feature and what are they willing to pay for it?

Interviewer: That's a good overview. Do you think customers will want it?

You: There have been a few different cell phone input devices over the years. Small and large keypads similar to those originally found on phones have been successful. Apple's iPhone and others have had some success with a touch screen although some keyboard users prefer the feel or real keys. Pen based devices, such as the one Palm Pilots used never really caught on in the mainstream because using them required a learning curve. Customers will want this device if it's as easy to use as a full keyboard and requires no additional learning or tradeoffs. Otherwise it may encounter some adoption headwinds.

Interviewer: That's a good phrase – you're already talking like a consultant. What about the channels?

You: We have a strong relationship in place with most of the OEMs, I assume, and they can rely on us to supply parts for their phones. Unless the competitor introducing this device can instill a similar sense of trust, they will have a hard time selling it to the OEMs.

Interviewer: What if end users are really crying out for it?

You: I don't know how likely that will be until it's already in a few phones that they can test. Suppliers, such as our client, that don't interface directly with end users don't have many options to advertise their products directly to them. Intel does a good job at this, but there are no other examples I can think of.

Interviewer: To step back for a minute, can you summarize where we are in the case?

You: We took paths. One, determine if they can actually pull this hologram keyboard off and two, if so, determine if and how we should react. On the first, we have anecdotal evidence that the OEMs will only adopt the new device if customers really need it and it is a risky bet to be a first mover in such a change. And we still haven't looked at the production costs or supply constraints.

Interviewer: We've done some research and have determined that that they can produce it for the same price as existing keyboards and they have two suppliers in China that can produce them. We also believe that one of the major OEMs, which has seen its market share erode considerably in the last couple of years, is willing to take a gamble in the hopes of a big payoff that could bring them back into the market.

You: So we can assume that the hologram company can build and deliver their product. Then we're in the second half of our initial work plan, which is to determine the effects to us and how to react. With that information, we can take two views on the situation. First, in the near term, will we lose revenue from the single sale to the OEM that is looking to take a gamble? Second, if it starts to become a popular option, how can we react in the long-term?

My sense from the setup of the case is that the CEO is most worried about the latter, although we can do the math to determine the short-term losses if he likes.

Interviewer: Let's focus on the long-term.

You: Given the iPhone and Palm Pilot devices we discussed earlier, it seems safe to say that this is an industry of constant innovation. So we have three options. First, keep our current keypad device and find a niche in the industry for which it best fits a need that we can defend. Second, copy what our competitors are doing. Third, out-innovate them. These are not mutually exclusive options. We can do all three. If we start at the last one, are they making major R&D investments in new ideas?

Interviewer: They are not. Should they?

You: I can't think of a high tech business that can survive over the long-term on a single product without any investment in innovation. So, yes, they need to invest. They can do R&D in-house or acquire smaller firms with innovative new ideas – big pharmaceuticals are doing more of that, for example.

Interviewer: Anything else?

You: The first option I mentioned is still viable, at least in the short term. Are there customer segments for which a keypad is the best option? A lot of people type into their phones while walking or riding the subway – the hologram keyboard won't work for them. So let's find the segments for which we best fit a core need and focus on keeping our position there.

Interviewer: OK, good thoughts. Thanks for coming in.

Feedback

This was a case that focused on big picture thinking and the interviewer waved away any suggestions of pulling in data or doing analyses. Sometimes second round cases can be more this way: a partner in the firm may be thinking over a problem that one of his client CEOs mentioned on the phone earlier in the morning and wants an opportunity to hear your take on it. There's no data yet; there's no team on the ground gathering it. Of the three suggestions given as feedback in the previous case, this time you included all of them.

- One area of improvement might be to stay focused on the big picture and focus only on the few ideas that will really impact the outcome. While you did this well in this case (and it is hard to know upfront how much detail the interviewer wants to get into), we spent a lot of the case time talking through the steps of the value chain when the interviewer ultimately wanted to move beyond those details. As a basic guideline, pulling in the value chain structure early on was a great idea and was used well here. However, you could read the interviewer (or explicitly asked them) if they wanted to dive in deep into that part of the analysis or focus on the second half of your initial setup: if and how to react to the threat. That's a small note though. Overall, the case went very well.

Sample dialogue #3: Determining how to increase profits

Interviewer: I've recently been working at a client in the southwest that operates a factory where "artists" manufacture oil paintings in a production-line system. The sell in the US and don't want to go international. They want to know how to increase their profits. What should we tell them?

You: *[Your thought process: summarize case, verify specific objective, and get a sense what the client's products are — these will inform your structure.]* Got it. Do they only sell oil paintings, or is there a larger set of products?

Interviewer: They only do oil now, but are thinking of moving into watercolors and sculptures.

You: *[As shown in Exhibit 6-6, the profit tree can be built for an entire firm or per product. Let's build for their current product and for both possible new product options.]* Let's start by seeing if there's room to increase their profits with the current product mix and then scope out possibilities for additional revenue streams.

Interviewer: Sounds good.

You: Is there a specific target they want: a 5% increase or 20%?

Interviewer: No specifically, but in our early pitch to the client, we said we try to achieve results that are 10x our fees. We're charging the client $500k for this engagement.

You: OK, so we're looking to increase their bottom line by $5 million or more. Before we jump into the details, what's their strategic direction?

Interviewer: Where are you going with that?

You: Where do they want to be in 5-10 years? As the world's top producer of fine art, for example? The reason I ask is that, especially as we start considering adding new products to their portfolio, that our incremental steps now directly help them towards a larger end goal. $5 million would be great to find for them by any means, but let's make sure that it doesn't steer them away from larger opportunities. *[The interviewer doesn't say anything, but is taking notes, so you keep talking.]* For example, if IBM had offered Bill Gates $5 million for his operating system back in 1980 instead of the royalty payment that he negotiated for, he may have taken it, but then there wouldn't have been a Microsoft.

Interviewer: I like how you're bringing in the analogies from another industry. These guys have no noble end goal like being the highest quality producer of fine art. I'm not sure I'd call what they do 'fine art' anyway...

You: *[Feeling comfortable with the case and sensing a good rapport with the interviewer, you take a bit of a gamble and stand up and walk over to the white board.]* Is it OK if I work off the whiteboard?

Interviewer: Please do…

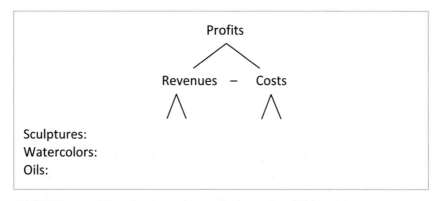

Exhibit 7-2 A profit tree for the art firm, as drawn on the whiteboard

You: If we just focus on the near-term opportunities, we want to know what our profits would look like for watercolors and sculptures. And we also want to look at the oil paintings division and see how we can improve profits there. So let's start with a simple profit tree. *[You draw the tree shown in Exhibit 7-2.]* It sounds like they're running a very efficient oil painting factory — much more efficient than I imagine their competitors are doing. So if you held a gun to my head right now and asked for an answer, I would have to say: you've got a secret recipe for extracting money out of oil paintings. Can you make the production line more efficient by 5%? Sure. But if you really want more income, what you need to do is sell more paintings or take that secret formula to other areas. But let's investigate and see if the facts bear that out. *[If you have a hypothesis about where the real value is, then say so. Be "80/20". But clarify that you will use the facts to verify those assumptions.]*

Starting with sculptures, let's look at the revenue potential there. When can structure our revenue as "price * volume", but before we get there, let's just ask how big the total sculpture market is in the US and how much of that total pie the top 2-3 players have. This should give us a sense of what our potential is. Do we have a value for those two elements?

Interviewer: No… but go ahead and make an estimate.

You: Sculptures aren't as popular as oil paintings — especially handmade sculptures. I hardly ever see them actually. How big is the oil painting market and what's our share there?

Interviewer: About $3 billion and we have a 1% share.

You: *[You write: "Size: $3B Share: 1%" in the oils line under revenue.]* So we have $30 million in revenue in oils. Just based on my own experiences, I'd say the market for sculptures is at most 10% the oil market. If we get the same 1% share there, we'd be talking at most $3 million in revenue. That's probably too low for us to push unless nothing else comes up. Let's sidetrack it and move on to watercolors. *[You write: "Size: <$300M Total rev $3M?" in the sculpture line.]*

Interviewer: OK. That's sounds like a reasonable estimate. Indeed, the watercolor market is similarly small.

You: Then going back to the initial set of options, let's see if we can get higher profits from the oil paintings. I'd look at revenue and costs. Here I'd ask, can we increase our revenues? Can we increase prices or volume? On the costs side, can we be more efficient with our production line or capital investments? Let's start with revenue. How are we priced relative to other oil painters?

Interviewer: Our prices tend to be in the bottom quartile of the market.

You: That's I'd expect because I assume our buyers know that the paintings are made in assembly-line style and the competitors' paintings are individual works?

Interviewer: That's right. We're very clear about our process in our marketing.

You: Our total revenues are $30 million in oils. What's our average price?

Interviewer: About $750 a painting and we sell directly to the end customer.

You: Now let's do some volume calculations. Are there multiple product segments worth considering, or do they mostly have just one style of painting at one price point?

Interviewer: There is some variation in price and distribution channels, but not worth segmenting.

You: *[You do the math on a corner of the whiteboard: $30,000,000 / 750.*
An easy way to do this is: $30,000,000 / (3/4*1,000) = $30,000 * 4/3]
40,000 paintings sold annually.
[Next step in the math is 300,000,000 people in the US / 40,000. Remove the common zeroes and you have: 30,000/4]
That's roughly one painting for every 7,500 people in the US…
[Roughly assuming 2.5 people per household, 7.5/2.5 = 3]
…or one for every 3,000 households every year. Given that this is a luxury art item, I'd imagine those are very high volume numbers.

Interviewer: I'd agree.

You: We could do analyses on the pricing, but given our value proposition, they sound like they're in the right ballpark. We could dig deeper into any of the levers we've discussed so far, but at a 30,000 foot level, it looks like costs are the only major bucket left to consider. Our options to enter other product markets seem limited, our oil painting volumes are exceptionally strong, and our pricing seems to be where we'd expect. Of course, having said that, it may be that we created new demand for oil paintings when we entered that market. I can't imagine that before we entered, someone else was selling that many paintings. So maybe that will bring us back to sculptures: before we assumed we would take competitor demand away. Now perhaps there's evidence that we can create new demand.

Interviewer: But we still only have 1% market share in oils so we haven't significantly shifted the overall market size there.

You: True. So let's look at costs. I'd look at variable costs and fixed costs. What are our variable costs per painting?

Interviewer: About $200.

You: And total fixed costs?

Interviewer: They amount to about 2-3% of revenue.

You: Those both seem very reasonable to me. We're already making good profits: $550 margin per painting and 40,000 paintings: $20 million a year on the bottom line. Unless I missed something, I'd say this company is already doing exceptionally well.

Interviewer: I agree, we couldn't find any major opportunities either.

You: So this was a trick case?

Interviewer: No, not a trick. You covered all the major areas and made the right assumptions. In the real world, there aren't always easy nicely-packaged answers to every question!

Feedback

It was a great idea in this case to draw the structure out on the whiteboard. It really seemed to pull the interviewer into the case and created an environment more like a team problem-solving than an interview. Of course, such a move has its risks and reading the interviewer to get a sense of how well it will work out is always a good idea.

In this case, you kept focusing on the 20% of the problem that gave 80% of the results: without getting stuck in the details, you kept the problem-solving pace moving along with reasonable assumptions and estimations and a solid overall structure. Of course, you could have gotten to the answer quicker by just looking at the oil painting revenues and costs up front, but there was a good discussion of other revenue streams that could have uncovered some ideas and really helped to build out the overall dialogue.

8   *Behavioral interviews*

Case interviews are just one part of the interview process. Many applicants do well in their cases, so the quality of your past experiences and how well you're able to discuss them will have a large impact on your success during the behavioral interview. Try to impress your interviewer by demonstrating that you're an accomplished leader with some interesting stories to tell.

A good approach to behavioral interviews is to have three or four stories from your past experiences worked out ahead of time. Then when your interviewer asks you a tough question such as "tell me about a time when you did something outside of your comfort zone", you don't have to think through everything you've done in your entire life, you just have to think which story will answer the question best.

You need to have an interesting set of past achievements and work experience to do well here though; no amount of practice and polishing can make up for a lack of substance. Choose your stories wisely. Do they show off your best qualities? Do they highlight your own personal achievements and not just the achievements of the group that you happened to be in? Teamwork and modesty are important, but you don't want your interviewer to be unimpressed with what you have done or unsure whether you can make a unique contribution to any team that you join.

Be honest about what *you* did. Interviews are not the time to be humble.

In a given round of interviews, you may have two or three different interviewers. It's best not to tell the same story twice since they'll meet afterwards and compare notes. They are looking for people who have accomplished many different things. So if you only have three stories to tell going in then in the third interview you have to tell your last story no matter what question they ask!

Practice your stories and practice adjusting each one to answer a number of different questions. Most stories should have a leadership element and demonstrate that you work well with other people. Even if they don't explicitly ask for evidence of those things, the interviewers are definitely looking for that.

Just as you bring structure to case interviews, you can bring structure to behavioral interviews too. For the question, "what are your strengths?", a good structured answer might start out as follows. "Three things come to mind: I'm entrepreneurial, outgoing, and hardworking. For the first one, I ran my own business for three years..." Conversation structure simply means laying out a roadmap of where you are going to take the conversation up front and then following each path individually.

Adapt to the interviewer's style. Are they quiet and pensive or loud and outgoing? Are they interested in every detail or only concerned with the big picture? Do they like small talk and side stories or do they just want to get to the point? Adjust your own personality to match their style and subconsciously they'll be more likely to like you.

Some pointers as you choose and develop your stories:

- It doesn't matter what you've done, but how you did it (and why you did it).
  - Be extremely passionate about the big events in your career and life.
  - You have to have done something with those things in a way that no one else would have done.
- You need to have taken on a number of leadership roles, even if you weren't officially appointed as the leader.
- You need to have understood others' feelings and taken them into account.
- Refresh your memory with all of the key facts and dates of your stories.
- Structure your stories in the format of Situation, Complication, Resolution.
  - Spend a minute detailing the situation at the start: what was the nature of the organization or industry at the time?
  - Then detail the complication as quickly and precisely as possible. Why was the problem that arose meaningful? How many people were affected by this change? What was at risk?
  - Finally, spend the majority of your time discussing how you resolved the problem. If you were on a team, what was your part? How would the events have unfolded differently had you knot been there?
- Think about the high-level strategic actions that your previous employer has undertaken in the last few years, such as mergers, divestures, or entering new markets. Why did they perform these actions? Consider the forces that affect and define the industry and the strategies of the major players in that industry.

Some advice to be taken with a grain of salt: as Robert McNamara (the Secretary of Defense during most of the Vietnam War) said in the documentary *Fog of War*: "don't answer the question you've been asked; answer the question you *wished* you'd been asked". If you spin a question in a slightly different way, it may make the answer obvious.

Leadership

All consulting firms – like all MBA programs – want to hire leaders. They all look for applicants who have been leaders in their past experiences and who show potential to develop quickly into greater leadership roles in their future careers. So what does it mean to be a leader and how can you demonstrate leadership in your interviews?

- Show leadership in the details
  - Most candidates that are applying to consulting firms are in the early stages of their careers. Most can't claim to have led an entire business unit of a large firm through a major transformation process. And even if you have, simply stating that fact is not enough.
  - Regardless of the size or capacity of the experiences you've had, look through the details for elements of initiative, providing others with direction, or handling a difficult situation.
- Show diversity in your stories
  - If leadership is in the details, one of the key details is being able to demonstrate it in a range of diverse experiences. Taking a pivotal role in your friend's startup during college, during a new product development at work, and as a keyboard player in a five-piece band on the weekends gives much more dimension to your candidacy as a potential leader in the future than three stories from the same company and position.
  - Consulting firms want to know that your leadership potential extends beyond your level of comfort in one particular area. Demonstrate that you can step into a new role without much previous experience in the field and proactively become a guiding force. Leadership in an area where you don't have the luxury and comfort of years' of previous experience can be much more insightful and detail-rich than leadership in your area of expertise.
- Servant leadership can be a powerful approach
  - Robert Greenleaf introduced the model of the servant leader in his 1977 book, which was inspired by Herman Hesse's 1932 book, *Journey to the East*. In *Journey*, the servant of a pilgrimage, after keeping the troupe intact and in good spirits through song and support, disappears, leaving the group to disintegrate into disarray. Ultimately, despite his official position, he was the team's leader; without him, nothing could be accomplished. The servant leader is someone who is driven by a desire to further the collective interest of the group rather than to simply acquire title and authority for themselves.
  - The powerful element of the servant leader position is that you don't need an official leadership title to display those qualities and further, such titles can even impede your ability to do so. Consultants often have no official authority in an organization, yet, by developing the trust and confidence of those who do, they can be tremendous catalysts for change (and they often prefer to receive no public credit for their work).

9   *Exercises to practice structuring (to do on your own)*

These exercises will give you some practice building structures around nebulous problems. Since there are no right or wrong answers, it may be beneficial to do them on your own and then compare your structures with others' or with some of the suggestions given at the end of the chapter.

Most people learn by doing. As an example, reading a book on strategy will likely be of limited use on its own in making you a better strategic thinker. But reading such a book while you are in the process of deriving a corporate strategy will give you multiple benefits. First, you will may recognize you are missing tools and knowledge to effectively handle the challenge you are facing. Your mind will then have an immediate context in which to place those tools and knowledge. Second, you will be able to try out and test the ideas with your own hands, allowing you to better absorb the subtleties and difficulties of their application. Therefore the next time you encounter such a situation, you will already have a multidimensional and meaningful context to use as a starting point. The ideas that you learned are much more likely to stick with you and you are much more likely to be able to know when and how to apply those tools in the future.

The ideas in Chapter 6 may seem either obvious or abstract on first reading, but the ability to absorb and benefit from them may only come from testing them in exercises or in a real situation. Hopefully the practice exercises and cases in this chapter and the next will give you a sufficient context in which to apply them. The practice exercises are good starting points in thinking about structuring case problems and are also very similar to the back-of-the-envelope/estimation problems that consulting firms occasionally give (often to undergraduates applying for analyst positions in lieu of a full case).

These types of exercises are easy to invent, so don't stop here. As you're reading the *Wall Street Journal* or *Business Week*, see if a title or a thought in an article presents an undefined problem that you can do the same type of exercise with. If GE is considering divesting one of its business units, build a framework to uncover all of the drivers that may be the reason, even if only in your head. You can also do these exercises with things you see around the room: how would you structure the set of reasons why people might choose to use pens over pencils, for example?

As you practice these exercises and build a method you can use in any situation and in any case, don't worry too much about being MECE. It's important to be MECE, but not to the extent that it blocks your creative thinking or constrains your ability to try out different ideas. You could easily divide most of these exercises into "positive forces and negative forces" or "internal and external issues" at the start. They may be MECE, but they will rarely give you any real insight into the problem.

Problem (Example):

What are the drivers for determining how many pages a book should have?

← (Start with a picture to help you visualize key elements of the situation. You may cringe at this approach, but at least give it a chance before deciding against it!)

Now brainstorm some ideas using your picture as a cue (you may want to do it on your own before reading these sample "solutions"):

- There should be enough pages to hold the content that the writer needs.
- There is the reader's perception: more pages mean more value. Book purchasers generally believe that if there are more pages, then it is more likely that the book has the answer to their question or need.
- Books have to be published in 16-page increments for binding reasons.

There may be some drivers we missed but one possible structure (which appears to be MECE) is:

Number of pages

Author's needs   Publisher's needs   Readers' needs
- Content   - Binding (16-page increments)   - Perception of value

Once you have such a structure in place (and a driver for each of the three branches), you're well on your way. Now you can look at each of the branches individually and ask if there is anything to add. This makes it much easier to come up with ideas than it was before we drew the tree. For example, when you consider which readers' needs may influence book length, their desire to keep the price of the book low immediately appears an obvious driver. For publisher needs, there may be a maximum limit on the number of pages their machine can handle and so on.

The best and most intuitive frameworks have a clear flow to them where you can see a natural progression among the components. Often the flow is the value chain as it is here. Books follow the value chain of creation (authors), manufacture (publishers), distribution, and purchase (readers). In this case, perhaps distributors (such as Amazon or other bookstores) might need to be included: can their shelves or computer systems can only handle books up to a certain page limit? Here, since we assume that no such distributor limits exist, we can decide not to include such a branch.

Create your own structure for these problems; example solutions are given on page 64.

- Our client washes the windows of skyscrapers using an external elevator device that drops from the top of the buildings. What are some ways to make washing windows safe hundreds of feet above the street?
- How can we improve our product's promotion/advertising?
- How can we improve our product's placement on store shelves?
- How would you disaggregate the factors that would determine where the best location along a river is to build a bridge?
- A mining company has purchased a plot of land in Canada with magnesium ore beneath the surface. They want to know whether to mine for the ore.
- Your client uses trucks to move inventory from the manufacturing plant to three separate warehouses. What are the drivers you could look at to ensure that they are using their trucks optimally?
- There's a man standing on the street corner wearing a green shirt. Why?
- How would you determine if a public housing project is successful (such as an apartment complex for which the government subsidizes the tenants' rent)?
- Total US consumer credit card debt was \$3.0 trillion in 2007 and grew at 5% from 2006. Quantitatively disaggregate credit card debt into 2 or 3 key sub-drivers, for example: Debt = x*y*z or Debt = a+b+c.

74

A few possible solutions / suggestions to the exercises

For all of these questions, there are dozens of possible answers; the sample suggestions are included here just to stimulate discussion.

How can we improve window washer safety? Drawing a picture of the scenario will help stimulate ideas here. First, why are we putting people in such precarious situations? Your tree might start with human versus robot solutions. For human solutions, there are the components of keeping the scaffolding safe and keeping the human safely on the scaffolding.

How can we improve our promotion/advertising? You might draw some of the possible advertising we're doing now: TV ads, print ads, internet, and billboards. Imagine who's looking at them and when. Which audience and location fits the product best? One structure might simply be to segment the customer base and evaluate what's important to them. You can segment by demographically, geographically, behaviorally, and other ways.

Product placement. You might draw the shelves with the product on it. Again, this could be a customer segmentation issue: who sees our product and what's important to them? And for the store: how high is the shelf? What products is it next to? What does our product look like and does it catch their eye? Which stores sell our product?

What factors would you consider in determining where to build a bridge? This should lend itself well to a drawing. How wide is the river you're trying to cross – is it narrower in some areas? Are there other bridges? Where are the roads that you'd have to connect to? What two areas does the bridge connect and is there a need to make that connection? Possible structure might be: river/environmental factors and people factors. After all, bridges are the solution to a man versus nature problem.

Environmental factors could include river and non-river factors. River factors would then include salinity of water (high salt content could rust the bridge faster), usage of the river by boats, depth, breadth, or strength of the current. Non-river factors might include wind, weather, and soil viability. High wind or rain areas might create unnecessary bridge design complications.

People factors might include a need for a bridge, the roads to connect it to, willingness to pay, competition or substitutes, and seasonal traffic patterns. By simply creating the first couple levels of the tree (environmental factors and people factors), the number of possible drivers to the situation increases greatly. Would we have been able to think of checking for high salt content before we created even this simple tree?

Magnesium mining. You already know this structure: they should mine simply if it will be profitable. On the cost side, you have the fixed costs associated with opening a mine, including the capital investments in mining equipment and salaried workers. You have variable costs, which include hourly labor, tools, and distribution costs. Revenue equals price of the ore times the amount that we can extract annually. On the volume side, it may also be worth checking what market share we will have globally to see if adding this new pipeline of ore into the world markets will lower the price by substantially increasing supply.

How would you optimize the truck route? You can start by optimizing the physical route they take and optimizing what they carry between points on that route.

Man on the street. There's probably no correlation between the green shirt and the street corner. For the street corner, he's either there with a purpose or no purpose. If a purpose, he's either waiting for something to happen to him (such as being picked up or handed a package) or for the chance to do something (such as sell tickets to the St. Patrick's Day Parade). If no purpose, perhaps he's lost or recently escaped from the Green City mental asylum and is confused where he is. The green shirt may simply have been the first one he picked out of his closet in the morning.

Success of a public housing project. You could start by looking at the different stakeholders and defining success for each one. For the builder, it's economic success. For the government, it's ultimately successful if the value of the benefits noticeably outweighs the costs.

The value of the benefits is to give families an affordable and safe place to live with the prospect of increased future salaries and income taxes. To calculate the value, you might analyze a sample of the residents before moving in and two years afterwards: Has their household income level changed? Has their exposure to crime decreased?

Total US credit card debt. Since US credit card debt is owned by the US population, a good start is to disaggregate into amount per person * number of people:

$$\$3{,}000{,}000M = \text{US population} * \frac{\text{Credit card debt}}{\text{per person}} = 300M * \$10{,}000$$

From there, you could disaggregate the \$10,000 further into old debt (\$9,500) versus new (\$500) based on the 5% growth rate in the previous year. New debt could be further broken into: new debt = amount charged * % not paid back. For example: = \$5,000 * 10%.

Again, there are many equally valid approaches and probably no right or wrong answers. The point of the exercises was just to give you a method to structure nebulous problems and a way to practice the method in your spare time. If you found it useful, it's easy to invent many more scenarios.

10   *Example cases (to do with someone else)*

Always practice cases with a partner – don't just read them! What may appear obvious from looking over the solution may be very hard to find when you have to search for it; building a structure that will let you find the answer in any situation is the key to solving cases. It also takes practice to develop the vocabulary and confidence to build a coherent conversation around the cases.

There are many other resources for further example cases. Just about every book on case interviewing has them. Consulting clubs at MBA schools often have a large database of cases online, as given to former students in actual interviews. And finally, many firms have sample cases posted on their websites (just Google: <firm name> "case interview").

A few different chart types are included here. It's critical to be familiar with different charts and the type of data that they convey. Whenever you see a chart in an interview, take a minute to talk over what it says: what do the data points represent (people, sales…)? What do the axes represent? What can you infer from the charts that may not be explicitly stated?

The charts for the cases are included at the end of the chapter so the interviewer can hand them to the candidate without revealing any of the case notes.

Thirteen cases are included here. The average applicant probably practices fifteen to twenty cases before their interview. If you're not a business school student or you're in an MBA program that doesn't do a lot of case studies as a part of your coursework, you should consider practicing more – some interviewees do sixty or more.

If you don't have a business background or haven't had much exposure to terms such as revenues, costs, levers, contribution margin, break-even point, return on equity, or similar, then consider practicing more cases to become comfortable with the language and tools of the trade. The ten cases here should give you a basic introduction to most of these fundamentals.

The 4 cases that have stars (☆) are my favorites. I've given these cases over the last couple of years to many students and find that they almost always help uncover key areas for improvement. Make sure you have a friend give the cases to you, though – again, if you just read the solutions, you will get very little value from them.

At the end of this chapter is a sample evaluation form. It may be similar to the evaluation forms that some of the consulting firms give their interviewers to use. The form is provided as a reference point in case you find it useful.

After finishing a case, take a few minutes to review how well you did. Ask yourself what you would change if you had to redo it. Would you use a different initial structure? Could you explain your thoughts more concisely? Also as a practice interviewer, giving feedback on these areas can be very helpful.

| Case 1: | American Bridge Corporation | Difficulty: Easy |

Problem Statement:

Our client, American Bridge Corporation, owns and operates 10 toll bridges in the American southwest. One of the bridges, the Santa Maria River Bridge, is much more profitable than the others. Our client wants to know why it is more profitable and whether the secret behind the higher profitability is replicable to the other bridges.

(Side note for interviewer – 1 possible structure that they could use):

The objective is profits; their structure should be the profit tree from the Valuation Framework in Exhibit 6-6. After that, the key insight is that "product mix" is the key driver: trucks are more profitable customers and the Santa Maria Bridge simply sees more truck traffic.

Insights, facts, and data:

* Release the following information only upon candidate inquiry.

Insights:

- Revenue comes entirely from tolls. Exact total revenue is unavailable.
- Tolls (price)
  - $1 for a car and $2 for a truck.
- Total number of vehicles that cross daily (volume or units)
  - Total volume is 1,000 vehicles per bridge per day for all 10 bridges.
- Fixed costs
  - We have long-term leases on the bridge locations. Our debt payments are identical for all 10 bridges. There are no other fixed costs.
- Variable costs
  - Variable costs = bridge upkeep per vehicle. Examples of such costs are resurfacing, painting, and rust-proofing. Costs are $0.25 for a car and $0.50 for a truck for all 10 bridges.
  - The candidate should note that trucks have a higher profit margin.
- The candidate should propose that the Santa Maria has a higher ratio of trucks to cars than the other bridges – which is the correct answer.

Interviewer: don't proceed until all of the above facts have been presented, even if you have to lead the candidate slightly to get them to ask the right questions.

Conclusion:
"How would you summarize your findings to the CEO?"   This is a simple case; it should be summarized in 15-30 seconds. Make sure they answer both of the initial questions: profit is higher because the percentage of vehicles that are trucks is higher and it is likely not replicable because changing the ratio of trucks to cars is not a lever we can pull (it's potentially possible if we consider building truck stops by the bridges or lower truck tolls in some locations).   After the case, hand them the sample notes and structure towards the end of this chapter. They can compare it with their own and use it as part of a "post-mortem" analysis. Their page of notes doesn't have to resemble the sample one: there are many ways to get to the solution. But it may help them consider ways to improve for the next time.

| Case 2: | DRY Soda Company | Difficulty: Easy |

Problem Statement:

Our client is DRY Soda, a niche manufacturer of all-natural, caffeine-free carbonated beverages that aims to compete with both cola products and champagne. They recently saw a major uptick in their sales and want us to figure out what caused it and how they can recreate it in the future.

(Side note for interviewer – 1 possible structure that they could use):

The objective is to diagnose changes in volume. The 4 P's is the recommended starting structure. The key to this case is that the demand for our product has always been very high: the only thing that changed was our ability to increased production to better meet demand. All of the questions on this page should lead to no clues; if they ask a question similar to the one at the top of the next page, then they've cracked the case.

Insights, facts, and data:

* Release the following information only upon candidate inquiry.

Insights:

- Has the company gone through any inorganic growth recently (acquisitions, joint ventures)?
  - No.
- Has the **product** changed?
  - No. Suppliers have been consistent and the number of products offered has remained the same.
- Have our customer needs changed, causing our **product** to become a better fit for them? For example, overall market size has grown in the soda market or we have seen a seasonal spike?
  - No. There has been no change in the overall market size and no seasonal spikes.
- Have we changed our marketing or **promotional** tactics?
  - No. We have not invested any more money into advertising. The quality and quantity of our advertising has not changed in any way.
- Have we increased the **placement** of our product? For example, introduced new distribution channels or expanded our geographic reach?
  - No.
- Have we changed our **price**? Or have our competitors changed their price?
  - No. There have been no price changes by us or our competitors.

- Have we increased our ability to manufacture the product?
  - Yes. We just opened a new production facility and that double our daily production. It turns out that demand for our product has been extremely high and we were simply not able to meet the demand before. We believe that the current demand is still much greater than our production capacity.

Interviewer: don't proceed until all of the above facts have been presented, even if you have to lead the candidate slightly to get them to ask the right questions.

Conclusion:
"What's your suggestion to the CEO?" "You asked us to investigate a recent spike in your sales volume. It turns out that we have been unable to meet the high demand for your products and it was simply the increase in our production capacity recently that caused the increase. At this time, we still believe we are not fully meeting demand and we propose considering further production capacity increases."

Case 3:	Flame Stripe Body Shop	Difficulty: Easy

Problem Statement:

Flame Stripe Body Shop, which operates in one location in the northeast, has grown significantly over the last few years. Last year, it saw record profits of $5 million, but this year it is looking at a $5 million loss.

It makes money by making structural repairs to cars. One functional group inspects the cars and gives price estimates. Other groups specialize in the various repairs or handle customer service, marketing, and billing.

It has 50,000 annual customers. How would you isolate the cause of the profit drop?

(Side note for interviewer – 1 possible structure that they could use):

The objective is profits; their structure should be the profit tree from the Valuation Framework.

Insights, facts, and data:

* Release the following information only upon candidate inquiry.

Insights:

- Revenues / price / volume
  - □ They are all stable. Average repair price is $500 and that hasn't changed.
- Fixed costs
  - □ Fixed costs are flat: no new capital expenditures. Fixed costs are $10 million / year.
- Variable costs
  - □ We'll get to that in a minute...

Interviewer: don't proceed until all of the above facts have been presented, even if you have to lead the candidate slightly to get them to ask the right questions.

Next step:

"What's our annual revenue?"

50,000 * $500 = $25 million

Next step:

"What was our cost per repair last year and this year?"

Last year:
$\pi = R - C$
$5M = $25M − 50,000*cost - $10M
$10M = 50,000*cost
Cost = $200

This year:
$\pi = R - C$
$-5M = $25M − 50,000*cost - $10M
$20M = 50,000*cost
Cost = $400

Next step:

"Why do you think average repair cost doubled?"

Start with a structure for variable costs, perhaps the value chain. Example response:

"It could be Raw materials or labor. I can't imagine packaging or distribution is relevant here. There may be some overhead and other costs associated with the finance and customer support groups, but that would likely be considered fixed costs."

Conclusion:

"Labor and material costs are the same per vehicle, but the new system of performing the diagnosis before the car is reviewed by the mechanics has caused a huge increase in misdiagnoses. This has led to cars moving around to different stations on the workshop floor and these inefficiencies and bottlenecks have caused the shop to stay open almost 24 hours a day and pay many of its workers overtime salaries. What's your suggestion to the CEO?"

There are a number of possibilities they should suggest, possibly including:
- Change the diagnosis system so that the diagnosis and price quote come from the mechanic.
- Put mechanics in the diagnoses jobs so misdiagnoses decrease.
- Rearrange the workshop floor to allow cars to move to different stations without disrupting the entire flow of traffic.

| Case 4: | Burgers-on-Wheels Market Entry | Difficulty: Easy |

Problem Statement:

Burgers-on-Wheels is a popular hamburger restaurant chain in Canada that is thinking of entering the US market. It follows the pizza delivery model of taking orders by phone and delivering the burgers to your house within 30 minutes; there are already a few similar restaurants in the US and they are growing in popularity. Burgers-on-Wheels is unsure of how to enter the US. There are two distribution options: building its own locations or partnering with an existing player, such as a pizza delivery chain.

It wants to know a few things: can it expand to the US? Should it? And if yes, by which method?

(Side note for interviewer – 1 possible structure that they could use):

The objective is profits: it should expand to the US if the expansion will be profitable. Of the 2 options, it should choose the most profitable. The candidate should start with a table collecting all the facts listed below. For each distribution option: the price, cost, and margin. No other structures are needed in this case.

Insights, facts, and data:

* Release the following information only upon candidate inquiry.

Insights:

- Price of burger (including delivery)
  - $5
- Cost of burger
  - Unavailable (depends on distribution option)
- Contribution margin per burger
  - If we build our own stores: $2.50.
  - If we partner with pizza firm: 70% of sale price.

- Once the candidate has the 3 data points above, ask them to calculate exact margin and cost per burger for both options:
  - Margin if we partner = 70% * $5 = $3.50. (So cost = $1.50)
  - Margin if we build stores = $2.50. (So cost = $2.50)

- Initial capital investment
  - If we build our own stores = $1 billion to build 100 stores; we plan to depreciate those costs over 20 years
  - If we partner there is no initial investment, but the cost of partnering = $5 million annually
- If they ask about the "5 Forces", that's a bonus, but they are not needed:
  - Threat of substitutes = low
  - Threat of new entrants = low
  - Power of suppliers = low
  - Power of buyers = low
  - Strength of competition = low

Interviewer: don't proceed until all of the above facts have been presented, even if you have to lead the candidate slightly to get them to ask the right questions.

Next step:

"What's our annual fixed cost if we build our own stores?"

Fixed costs here are just the annual depreciation values. Assume straight-line depreciation.

$1 billion / 20 years = $50 million annually

Next step:

"What's the break-even point when building our own stores becomes profitable?"

Break-even point = Fixed cost / contribution margin
$50M / $2.50 = 20 million burgers annually

Next step:

"What's the break-even point when partnering becomes profitable?"

Break-even point = Fixed cost / contribution margin
$5M / $3.50 = 1.43 million burgers annually

Next step:
"Assume 500 million meals are served annually by restaurants in the area we are looking at. Assume that customers who buy hamburgers buy 1 burger per order. Chart 1 has the details. Is this a good investment?" (Show them Chart 1).   First, they should talk through what the chart means. (See end of this chapter for all charts.)   Given it, we can calculate the current number of burgers sold by delivery annually: 500 million meals * 40% * 15% = 30 million burgers sold – that's the current market size.

Conclusion:
"What's your summary to the CEO?"   If we partner, we'd only need 11% of the total market (3.3 out of 30 million meals).   However, if we build our own stores, we'd need 66% market share (20 out of 30 million).   This is assuming we wouldn't create new demand; that we'd only steal share from competitors.   Partnering is viable; building our own stores is likely not, at least in the next few years.

Case 5:	Herbie's Snack Cakes	Difficulty: Medium

Problem Statement:

Herbie's is a manufacturer of snack cakes that distributes to retail outlets in North America. A recent analysis determined that for each box of its best-selling Product A sold, 80% of its customers also purchase Product B. The other 20% only purchase boxes of Product A. No customers purchase only Product B alone. The company asked us to determine if they should bundle the 2 boxes together instead of selling them separately. How would you think about solving this problem?

(Side note for interviewer – 1 possible structure that they could use):

This is a great example of a case for which memorizing frameworks ahead of time will not help you in a case interview. If you don't have a consistent, fundamentally-strong problem-solving method that you can apply to any problem, your head will likely start to spin when hearing a case introduction such as this one!

Starting with the fundamentals described earlier: the company should take the action if it will be profitable. So the objective is profits; their structure should be the profit tree from Exhibit 6-6.

The two main things that you're looking to hear:
- Profits = Revenue – Costs = volume * (price – variable costs) – Fixed costs
  - Since fixed costs will not change, we only have three drivers to consider: changes in sales volume, price, and variable costs.
- For volume, we want to know: of the 20% of our customers that will be affected by this change, how many will continue to buy our new double-size bundled box and how many will simply stop being our customers?
  - Note that volume from the 80% that purchase all 4 products will not be affected.
- Will we change our price?
- Will our variable costs decline?

If the candidate covers most of these points, but they don't cover them as succinctly, summarize that the only components we need to investigate are simply changes in volume, price, and variable costs.

Next step:

"Here are some details:" (Read off this data, stopping to ask the questions in bold.)

- Volume data:
    - Total number of customers: 1,000
    - Average annual purchase for the 80% that buy all products is 100 boxes of A and 100 boxes of B.
    - Average annual purchase for other the 20% is 150 boxes of A.
        - Our research indicates that of this 20%, if we make the change, 50% will stop purchasing all products from us. The other 50% will purchase 75 boxes of Product A and 75 boxes of Product B.
    - Ask: "What is our current total annual sales volume for A?"
        - $1,000*80\%*100 + 1,000*20\%*150 = 80,000 + 30,000 = 110,000$
    - Ask: "What is our *expected* total annual sales volume for A if we bundle?"
        - $800*100 + 200*50\%*75 = 80,000 + 7,500 = 87,500$
    - Ask: "What is our current total annual sales volume for B?"
        - $800*100 + 200*0 = 80,000$
    - Ask: "What is our *expected* total annual sales volume for B if we bundle?"
        - $800*100 + 200*50\%*75 = 80,000 + 7,500 = 87,500$
        - (Note that this has to be the same as A's expected sales volume since we're proposing to only sell them both together.)

Next step:

"Can you summarize what we've learned so far?"

A good answer would be something such as:
"If we only sell our products in a bundle, we will see about a 22,000 unit decline in A (about 20% of its current volume) and a 7,500 unit increase in B (about 10% of its current volume)."

A great answer would also include an insight such as:
"Assuming A and B have similar margins, this volume decline alone would represent about a 10% net decline in profits. For it to be worthwhile, we would have to be able to realize cost savings that could increase our margins by 10% or more. Even if we could do that, taking an action that would lose 20% of the sales of your core brand is a very risky move."

Next step:

"Assume that our prices will remain constant. Our current variable cost per box of A is \$4.50 and the variable cost per B is \$5.50. Both sell wholesale for \$12. If we bundle the two boxes, our total variable cost for the new box will be \$8 (it will be twice as large as the original Product A and B boxes) and it will sell wholesale for \$24. Will the bundling move be profitable?"

- Current contribution margin for box of A = \$7.50
- Current contribution margin for box of B = \$6.50
- Current net contribution for A =
    - 110,000 units * \$7.50 = \$825,000
- Current net contribution for B =
    - 80,000 units * \$6.50 = \$520,000
- Current net contribution for both = \$1,345,000

- Expected contribution margin for bundled box = \$16
- Expected net contribution for double-size box after bundling =
    - 87,500 units * \$16 = \$1,400,000

Therefore the answer is: "Yes, the bundling move would be profitable (at least initially, by these calculations).

Next step:

"What are some of the risks of the bundling move?"

The main risk is the 20% decrease in sales volume of the client's core brand. Risks associated with that effect include:
- Strengthening of competitors
    - Competitors will pick up the lost market share and could use it to strengthen their relationships with suppliers, distributors, and end users
- Loss of supplier leverage
- Decrease in customer loyalty
    - We can assume that B does not have the same customer loyalty levels as A and therefore the decline in A's availability could trigger a decline in overall customer loyalty to the company that would likely not be offset by the increase in sales volume of B.

Other risks include:
- Alienation of distributors
  - Even the distributors that typically carry both products will not appreciate the lack of ordering flexibility.
- Decrease in flexibility to respond to customer trends
  - If B increases in popularity over time, we will have no options available to adjust our product mix or allow distributors to adjust their orders.
  - We will also see a significant decline in ability to respond to seasonal trends.

Conclusion:

"**How would you summarize your findings to the CEO?**"

A good answer would recap the problem we're attempting to solve, summarize the answer, and then give a brief overview of the reasoning. For example:

"We determined that the bundling move would increase profits slightly, but we **recommend against** taking the action because it would require losing about 20% of the sales volume of your core brand, A. This move could empower competitors and alienate distributors. Customer brand loyalty to your other products is also are likely to be much lower. Therefore the move would leave you in a significantly weaker strategic position."

The best response will start with the final recommendation (whether they propose bundling or not).

Case 6:	Lemon-AID Stand	Difficulty: Medium

Problem Statement:

My nephew is running some lemonade stands where all of the profits will be donated to saving the rainforest. He runs 35 lemonade stands. The lemonade stands offer 4 major products: single cup drinks, lemonade party packs, cookies and snacks, and t-shirts. Business grew very fast in May and June but now growth has slowed and he wants us to work out a strategy to restore his top-line growth during July and August. How would you think about attacking this issue?

(Side note for interviewer – 1 possible structure that they could use):

The objective is revenue ("top-line growth"). If they propose a structure for increasing profits, re-read them the last 2 sentences of the problem statement.

Insights, facts, and data:

* Release the following information only upon candidate inquiry.

Insights:

- <u>What are the revenues or volume for each of our product types?</u>
  - [Show them Table 1 at the end of this chapter and move to the next question.]
- If they propose mergers, acquisitions, or other inorganic growth, rule out those options.
- Rule out geographic expansion / opening more stands.
- There are no specific growth projections.
- What are our prices / what's our pricing strategy?
  - We are priced competitively with no opportunity for change here.
- What are the margins per product?
  - All products are profitable. Beyond that, let's just focus on growing the top-line in this case.
- What are party packs?
  - These are packages that include a gallon jug of lemonade and 20 cups.
- How do they sell t-shirts?
  - T-shirts are hanging on the stands, but are not actively promoted.

> **Next step:**
>
> "What does the chart tell you? Where are our opportunities for growth?"
>
> They should easily observe that there is an opportunity with party packs and cookies and snacks: they have high growth potential and a significant revenue base. Cookies also have a diverse customer base.

> **Next step:**
>
> "As you can see, my nephew is currently segmenting the market in terms of his products. Is there a better way to segment the market?"
>
> The market could be better segmented in terms of customer types. At the top level, segmenting by individuals and businesses. The candidate should observe that the two product types we identified as having the greatest growth opportunities are sold to businesses. The next step they should propose is to further segment the business market: what are the different types of businesses, how much do they spend on our products, and what are the growth opportunities for each?

> **Next step:**
>
> "If we segment based on individuals and businesses. If we just consider those 2 for now, which of those two would you focus on and why?"
>
> - They can choose *either* 1 of the 2 options. Just check that they pick one solution and give their reasoning (instead of wavering between both options):
>   - Businesses have solid revenue base (~$115,000) with high growth
>   - Individuals have strong revenue base (~$190,000) with low growth
>
> Once they have proposed a course of action, show them Table 2.

> **Next step:**
>
> "What does this chart tell you? Where's our biggest growth opportunity?"
>
> - We have over 50% of the revenue that medium and large businesses spend on beverages already so growth opportunities may be limited.
> - We have very little of the small business beverage spend; this represents a large growth opportunity.
>   - If they say "large businesses", ask: "Do you think that our lemonade could be increased to *75%* of their total beverage spend?"
>   - If proposed, suggest avoiding new products at this time.

"If we can increase the amount that small businesses spend with us as a percentage of their total - to the same level that we have for medium and large businesses - what percentage would that increase our total top line by?"

- Correct answer: "About 10%." Let them use the following <u>approximations</u>:
    - If we achieve a little over 50% of the total small business beverage spend, we would see an increase of about <u>$15,000</u> in monthly revenues.
    - $15,000 / per month = $30,000 over two months. Our total 2 month revenues from Table 1 totaled about <u>$300,000</u>, so this would be a 10% increase.
    - A good candidate will also note that the $300,000 total represents a time when we were growing so the expected July-August revenues would be higher. Therefore the increase we realize may not represent a full 10% over July-August revenues.
    - Check that they don't divide $15,000/$144,000 to get to a 10% answer!
- If they give "20%" or "25%" as the answer, say: "That's just how much it would increase our Business customer revenue, how much would it increase our *total* top line?" (i.e. use the total top line value from Table 1.)
- If they give "4%" or "5%" as the answer, say: "Be careful: are you comparing the same time frames across each table?"

Next step:

"10% is a significant growth opportunity. Let's go after the small businesses. What would your next step be in doing that?"

- Ideally, the candidate would propose further segmentation of the small business market. A concern with small businesses is that reaching them could require more distribution channels, sales, and product transportation. Are there office parks with multiple small businesses that we can reach at one time? Are there existing beverage distributors that make regular visits to them that we can partner with? Is our pricing correct for small businesses?
- Encourage the candidate to propose a number of possible solutions to the unique problems that selling to this customer segment may present.

Conclusion:

"What's your 30-second overall recommendation to my nephew?"
A good response would start by recapping the problem we were asked to solve. Then saying we believe there is a potential for $30,000 in additional revenues in July-August by targeting small businesses that are currently vastly underserved by us relative to medium and large businesses.

Case 7:	King's Insurance Group	Difficulty: Medium

Problem Statement:

Our client is King's Insurance, a major insurance group. They have a number of offices around the country. They offer 4 types of insurance: fire, car, life, and renters' insurance. They're profitable and growing slowly, but the CEO wants to increase overall market share. The CEO believes she can increase share by increasing her sales staff but is unsure where to do so. There are 3 types of sales staff: office managers, renters' agents, and telemarketers. How should we proceed?

(Side note for interviewer – 1 possible structure that they could use):

The objective is market share (volume is also a valid objective). The short-term/long-term structure for increasing volume is one good starting structure. But in this case, the candidate should start with a table collecting all the facts listed below: for each product, the market share and margin (and possibly growth rates).

Insights, facts, and data:

* Release the following information only upon candidate inquiry.

Insights:

- Who are our competitors / what is their market share?
  - There are 4 players including us, each with a 25% market share, although market share differs by product line.
- Our market shares per product are:
  - Fire: 29%
  - Car: 28%
  - Life: 30%
  - Renters': 13%
- Our profits per transaction are:
  - Fire: $20
  - Car: $30
  - Life: $40
  - Renters': $70
- [Bonus points if they ask for product growth rates!]
  - Fire: 2-3% per year
  - Car: 3-4%
  - Life: 1-2%
  - Renters': 4-5%

- What do renters' agents do?
  - They work with local apartment buildings to build partnerships to create new customer leads. When someone new rents an apartment, the landlord suggests King's Insurance as the preferred renters' insurance.

Interviewer: don't proceed until all of the above facts have been presented, even if you have to lead the candidate slightly to get them to ask the right questions.

Next step:

The candidate should acknowledge that investing in renters' insurance may be best because of the high margins and room to grow market share.

"Let's focus on growing the market share for renters' insurance then. What else do you need to know?"

They should ask for the effectiveness of each of the 3 sales force types. When they do, show them Chart 1. (See end of this chapter for the chart.)

Next step:

"What does this chart tell you?"

Increasing the number of renters' agents will help us in our goal of increasing market share for renters' insurance. Increasing the number of telemarketers may also increase profitability, but that's not our goal in this case.

Next step:

"As a side note, assume the managers on this chart wait in the office for customers to walk in. The average store has two managers. What information would you need to determine whether adding more managers would be beneficial?"

Simply, how busy are the managers? What is the average customer wait time before being seen by a manager? What customer percentage enters the office and then leaves because the wait was too long? If two managers can handle the traffic, there is no benefit to adding more.

Conclusion:
"OK, assume that right now, in a few locations, the managers are completely busy with the current stream of customers entering their offices – they have no free time. What's your overall recommendation to the CEO?" Increase the number of renters' agents to build new customer leads in renters' insurance. This may also increase the stream of customers to our offices that are already very busy, therefore we may also need to increase the number of office managers in some locations.

Case 8:	Counter-Intelligence	Difficulty: Medium

Problem Statement:

Our client, Counter-Intelligence, manufactures surgical sponges with RFID tags embedded into them and a machine that can count the number of such sponges when they are all thrown into it.

Sponges are 6 inch square gauze strips that are used to control blood flow during hospital Operating Room (OR) procedures. Nurses typically count the sponges to be used in an operation before it starts and then again after it is finished. If a sponge is missing, the surgeon has to examine the patient and the entire room for it. The counting method is sometimes inaccurate, causing sponges to be left inside the patient's body. When that occurs, the hospital has to pay for a second operation to remove it. The counting method is also time-consuming, taking about 10% of the total time spent in the OR.

Our client's sponges and machine allow for an immediate and 100% accurate count of the sponges. They want to sell the counting machine for a nominal price and build their business model on selling the sponges. They have patents on their RFID sponges so no competitor can manufacture any similar product at this time. We want to determine a price that they should sell their sponges for.

Let's start by asking: **What are some of the drivers in determining the price?**

(Side note for interviewer – 1 possible structure that they could use):

The objective is price. The candidate's starting structure could resemble the price sub tree from the Valuation Framework.

You basically want to hear the candidate mention that they would find a baseline price based on the competitive products out there currently.

If they propose determining the cost of the sponges to set the lowest possible price, say that the price of each sponge is close to $0.

Next step:
"Here is some additional data:" (give this to candidate without them asking for it) • Old sponge price = $0.10 • Number of sponges used per operation = 20 • Total OR cost = $2,000 per hour (including nurses and surgeon salaries) • Average operation time = 1 hour • Frequency of a second operation to remove a sponge = 1% • If a second operation is needed, the frequency of a lawsuit = 10% "Given this data, let's calculate the Cost-Neutral Point (CNP) – the price point for our new sponge where it becomes more cost effective for hospitals to switch to our sponges. Is there any other data you need to make that calculation?"

Insights, facts, and data:
* Release the following information only upon candidate inquiry. *Insights:* • Cost of a lawsuit = $28,000 • Frequency of a second operation or a lawsuit with the new sponges = 0% • Same number of new sponges are needed per operation (20) • % of OR time spent counting when using new sponges = 0% Interviewer: don't proceed until all of the above facts have been presented, even if you have to lead the candidate slightly to get them to ask the right questions. They should calculate the CNP to be $12.50 per sponge. Example calculation:

With old sponges

Sponge cost	$2.00	*(Per operation)*
OR time spent counting	$200.00	($2,000*10%)
Cost of 2nd operation	$20.00	($2,000 * 1 * 1%)
Cost of lawsuit	$28.00	($28,000 * .1%)
Total cost	$250.00	

With new sponges

Sponge cost	20 * X	
OR time spent counting	$0.00	
Cost of 2nd operation	$0.00	
Cost of lawsuit	$0.00	
Total cost	$250.00	(same as above)
What is X?	$12.50	($250 / 20)

Next step:

"What additional factors may allow us to price the sponges above $12.50?"
 	
Here are some example responses:
    • Less likelihood of a second operation may provide more confidence and less pain for their patients.
    • Decrease of OR usage time by 10% may allow them to perform 10% more operations.
    • Lower malpractice costs in the future as lawsuits decrease.

Next step:

"What if the hospitals refuse to consider paying $12.50 per sponge? A recent survey showed they would consider paying only $1-$2."
 	
Here are some example responses:
    • Communicate the total value to them more articulately: the 10% OR savings time, for example, is an especially compelling argument.
    • Let them test the sponges at a $1-$2 price for 2 months so they can convince themselves of the value.
    • Advertise to create a demand from patients for the new sponges.

Conclusion:
"How would you summarize to the CEO?" As always, the candidate should repeat the case objective and then give the $12.50 price point suggestion. Then give the top 2-3 reasons why they chose this price point and 2-3 ideas to convince customers that it is the right price.

Case 9:	Boardwalk Whiskey	Difficulty: Medium

Problem Statement:

Our client, Boardwalk Whiskey, owns about 15% of the market share for whiskey in the United States. It wants to acquire Highland Whiskey that has a 10% market share. The only other major competitor has 30% share; the rest of the market is fragmented. The cost to acquire will be slightly more than it's worth as a standalone entity. Should Boardwalk make the acquisition?

(Side note for interviewer – 1 possible structure that they could use):

The objective is an acquisition. The best candidate would ask what our products are. Then they will ask why we want to make the acquisition. The candidate's starting structure could resemble the M&A sub tree from the Valuation Framework.

Insights, facts, and data:

* Release the following information only upon candidate inquiry.

Insights:

- What are our products?
  - □ We have 3 products, all of which are made in the same location: Boardwalk Regular that's our cash cow: it's profitable, has very strong market share, but is low growth. Boardwalk Gold is highly profitable. And Boardwalk Special, a niche brand similar to a microbrew, is marginally profitable.
  - □ Highland has a similar line of 3 products.
- Why do we want to do the acquisition?
  - □ Boardwalk believes there is a good cost synergy opportunity.
- What is the value of Highland? / What is the purchase price?
  - □ We believe we would pay the fair market price for Highland.
- Are there any legal issues that could prevent the merger?
  - □ No.
- Do we believe we can add value to Highland, such as through better management or revenue or cost synergy opportunities?
  - □ Yes; we'll look at those in detail in a minute.
- Is there a good cultural fit?
  - □ Yes.

Interviewer: don't proceed until all of the above facts have been presented, even if you have to lead the candidate slightly to get them to ask the right questions.

Next step:
"You mentioned cost synergies as a possible driver in this acquisition. What are some cost synergies we might be able to take advantage of?" A good answer would be to use the value chain to enumerate all of the possible cost buckets: • Raw materials / procurement • Manufacturing • Bottling / "packaging" • Distribution • Advertising • Customer support • Corporate overhead

Next step:
"Can you give recommendations for how we could find synergies in each of the costs you listed? Also, for each one, what is the potential for cost savings?" There's no right or wrong answer here. Example discussion might include: • Economies of scale for procurement: ingredients or bottles. Potential: low because each firm already has a large market share. • Combining manufacturing into a single facility. Is there excess capacity in one of the company's plants? Potential: high, but depends on the data. • Advertising. We would have 6 total brands: can we eliminate or reposition any of them? We could merge the marketing offices of both firms. Potential: medium/high. • Customer support. Probably not relevant in this industry.

Conclusion:
"Of all the cost synergies you discussed, let's say you had to choose one. You just met the CEO in the elevator and you have 30 seconds to pitch your suggestion to her."

Case 10:	Sigma Watches	Difficulty: Medium

Problem Statement:

Sigma watch company manufactures and markets mid- to high-end wristwatches. Watches are either sold through high-end retailers and independent jewelers or through private label partnerships with corporations. For example, they branded watches with the logo of a major airline that sold them through in-flight catalogs and to frequent flyers. Sigma is looking to grow in the United States, but their penetration in the 18-32 age bracket is lower than their competitors'. This is a high-margin and fast-growing age group and they want to capitalize on that.

How would you find the cause for the low market share and what can we do to fix it?

(Side note for interviewer – 1 possible structure that they could use):

The objective is volume (or "volume in the given market"). Thus, the candidate's best starting structure is the 4 P's. In Chapter 6, we mentioned that the 4 P's is the best structure for volume when you want to find drivers for low sales. Their structure could also resemble the short-term/long-term volume subtree from the Valuation Framework, but that may lead the candidate towards discussing levers to pull as opposed to figuring out the root cause of the issue.

Next step:

The candidate should start by walking through a structure to find the different drivers of low sales – ideally, using the 4 P's. If they don't do this immediately, the interviewer should lead them with:

"What might be some of the drivers for low sales in this market segment?"

- Product
  □ Do our watches meet the needs of the customers?
- Promotion / Advertising
  □ Does our advertising reflect the needs of the customers and the qualities of our watches in a way that effectively differentiates us from our competitors?
- Pricing
  □ Is our pricing competitive with the market leaders' prices?
- Placement
  □ Do the targeted segment shop at the stores or use the airlines that we are distributing through?

Next step:
"Here are some numbers. How many new customers do we need to reach our goal? (Assume the demographic values won't change over the next 3 years): • Our profit margin on watches is \$150. • There are 50 million people in the US in our target age range. • 60% of them wear watches. • Currently our market share among those who wear watches is 1%. • We want to get to 3% within 3 years. Answer: 600,000 new customers. They should calculate the size of the market: 30 million. We have 300,000 and want to grow to 900,000.

Next step:
"How much is that increase in customer base worth to us per year?" Answer: \$90 million (\$150 * 600,000).

Next step:
"The jewelers and retail stores that we distribute our product through are rarely visited by this target age range. Let's say we found a new store, StreetWear, that has 1,000 locations in the United States and its customer profile is almost entirely in the 18-32 age range. They sell watches. Here are some numbers: • Each store averages 20,000 unique customers in this age range per year. • The average customer purchases a new watch from this store every 5 years. In other words, 20% of the customers will purchase a watch every year. • The stores currently sell 4 types of watches. • If we were to sell in these stores, we would create a new style of watch that would be similar in price and product profile as their current watches. • Assume that if we were to sell our watches in these stores, ours and each of the 4 competitors' watches would sell equally well. Given these values, how many new watch sales could we expect through StreetWear per year? Would that meet our goal?" Answer: Yes, it would meet our goal. We'd see 800,000 new watch sales. 20,000/5 = 4,000 watches sold per year per store. We'd get 1/5 of those sales = 800 watches per store.

Next step:
"Assume it would cost us $30 million per year to create the new distribution and advertising channels necessary to meet our projected sales figures in these new stores. What would our total new profit be?" Answer: (Using the same $150 profit margin). Same value as calculated earlier: $90 million. 800,000 * $150 = $120 million. Then subtract the $30 million in new fixed costs.

Next step:
"So adding this sales channel seems like a good idea. What are some of the risks?" Some risks might include: • Brand erosion: selling in StreetWear could adversely affect our luxury brand reputation. • Backlash from our current sales channels for similar reasons. • Adding new distribution and advertising channels always carries a risk. This is a new customer segment for us: are we sure we understand them correctly? We have no experience advertising to this group.

Conclusion:
"What's your summary to the CEO?" One possible response: "We're still investigating the possible options, but it appears that by adding StreetWear as a new distribution channel, we can achieve our goal of increasing our market share in the 18-32 age group from 1% to 3% and see $90 million in new annual profits by doing so. Brand erosion is a central risk that we're considering as well as our ability to effectively market to this market segment. We'll push further with our investigation and get back to you in a few weeks."

Case 11:	Memphis Apparel	Difficulty: Medium

Problem Statement:

Our client, Memphis Apparel, owns the entire value chain from raw material production to the retail stores that they sell their clothing in. They have 500 retail stores in the United States, focused on high-quality clothing for women and kids. Each store also has a café that offers gourmet coffee and pastries. Profitability has declined in the past year and the CEO would like us to figure out why and introduce a plan for the next 5 years.

(Side note for interviewer – 1 possible structure that they could use):

The objective is profits. The candidate's starting structure could resemble the profit tree from the Valuation Framework.

Next step:

Before allowing the candidate to probe into the areas of revenue and costs, the interviewer should lead them with:

"The number of total retail stores (not just ours) has declined by 2% in the past three years in the US. What are some possible reasons for this decline?"

The candidate should build a structure to answer this question. One possible framework might be:

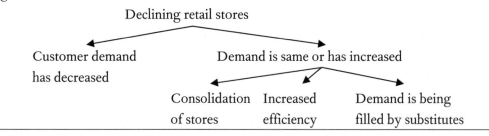

Next step:

Once they have built some structure for the above question (it doesn't have to be the same as the example framework given):

"The number of stores has decreased because of an increase of substitutes: megastores like Wal-Mart, who sell groceries, clothing, furniture, toys, and most everything else, have taken a lot of the demand once filled by retail stores. These megastores often also have cafés attached to them. Let's just consider the clothing and café components of their business. The megastores sell 50,000 articles of clothing per year each at an average price of $15. Their cost per item averages $5 plus 20% import taxes on that $5 (because the clothing is made overseas). Overhead is 33% of clothing revenue. Capital is a one-time cost of $800,000 (not an annual cost). And finally, their cafés generate $200,000 profit annually.

Retail stores have a similar structure, but they average 25,000 sales per year with a $20 per item average price; costs are $10. Everything else is the same.

What is the Return on Invested Capital (ROIC) for the megastores' café and clothing departments? ROIC = annual margin divided by initial capital cost."

Answer: 50% (Revenue = $750,000; Variable costs including overhead = $550,000; Contribution margin = $200,000. Add to that the $200,000 café profits and the one-time $800,000 capital investment returns $400,000 in profits per year.)

Next step:

"Without doing the calculation, do you think the ROIC for retail stores would be higher or lower?"

Answer: Lower (because sales are significantly lower and per-item margin and all other factors are similar).

Next step:

"What are some of the levers that our client could pull to increase their ROIC?"

Possible answers: Sell more, raise price, lower product costs, lower overhead, or increase café sales/prices. (These all come directly from the discussion above.)

Next step:

"Assume that cafés account for 90% of our client's profits. Let's try to increase the profitability of the café. How should we determine what products to carry?"

Again, the candidate should build a (profitability) structure to answer this question. We want to stock higher margin products, increase our volume, and lower our costs (such as overhead and labor or by centralizing procurement to purchase in bulk). Volume is perhaps the most interesting lever: the Valuation Framework has a list of ways to increase volume and almost all of them are relevant here.

Conclusion:

"How would you summarize to the CEO?"

Case 12:	Mr. Grill's Tech Support	Difficulty: Hard

Problem Statement:

Our client is Mr. Grill, a manufacturer of a sophisticated restaurant-level grill. Their device has become increasingly complex in recent years, with many new features being added. This increased complexity has decreased usability. They have been receiving a lot of tech support calls and we have been asked to find ways to reduce the tech support expenses.

When a tech support call comes in, a call center operator answers it. If the call center operator is unsuccessful in solving their problem, they dispatch a support person to visit the customer's kitchen. If a support person is dispatched or the call is solved on the phone, the problem is completely resolved; in other words, we don't need to worry about repeat calls. What do you want to know to get started?

(Side note for interviewer – 1 possible structure that they could use):

The objective is reducing tech support costs. The candidate's starting structure could be to disaggregate the problem into two options: improving the product to reduce incoming tech support calls and reducing the costs of handling each call.

Insights, facts, and data:

* Release the following information only upon candidate inquiry.

Insights:

- Can we change the product / can we doing anything to adjust the number of calls coming in / something similar?
  - No – we've been trying to get them to simplify the interface for a while, but it won't happen anytime soon. Every time they add a new feature, they receive a patent to add to their wall; that seems to be what they're most interested in.
- Cost of call center employee
  - $10/hour. [This should lead them to asking about time per call]
- Cost of field worker
  - $22/hour, including overhead.

- Average time spent per call
  - There are 2 types of call center operators; we call them Fast Franks and Careful Carissas. Fast Franks can handle about 3 calls per hour. Careful Carissas handle about 1 call per hour.
- Average time spent in the field per dispatch
  - When we dispatch a worker, they average 1 hour in the field.

With this information, it is clear that we would prefer spending up to 2 hours on a call if a field worker does not need to be sent out.

If the interviewer asks for the number of calls coming in, ask them why they want to know that information: we can't change the number (see above), so what will they do with it if you give it to them? If they ask for the ratio of field worker to call operator volume or costs, say it's very different for each operator and we'll get into those details later.

Next step:

"Who is more valuable to us, Fast Frank or Careful Carissa?"

Key insight: how many calls they answer in an hour isn't enough information; we also need to know how successful the Franks versus Carissas are in solving the problem on the phone (i.e. how often they have to send out a field operator).

Once they have this insight, show them Chart 1. (See end of this chapter for the chart.)

Next step:

"What does this chart tell you?"

Look for: do they talk through what the chart means? Do they ask what each point in the plot represents (annual averages per each employee)? Do they correctly interpret the axes?

Key insights: First, the employee in the top left is more valuable than the one in the bottom right.

If the candidate doesn't lean towards this, it's OK to ask them: "What is the average cost per call for the call center operator in the top left and the one in the bottom right?"

If they still have trouble after about 5 minutes, as a last resort, suggest: "We want to calculate the average cost per call; start with the number of calls solved in a 10-hour window and then calculate the total cost of handling those calls for the two operators we're interested in."

Number of calls solved in 10 hours for the top-left person (a "Careful Carissa")
= 10; but 30% need field operator trips (3 trips).
Total cost = $10*10 + $22*3 = $166
Average cost per call = $166 / 10 = $16.60

Number of calls solved in 10 hours for the bottom-right person (a "Fast Frank")
= 30; but 80% need field operator trips (24 trips).
Total cost = $10*10 + $24*22 = $628
Average cost per call = $628 / 30 = (approx) $21

Next step:

"Assume that the chart converges on 70% on the left and 20% on the right side. What does that tell us?"

No matter how long you spend on a call, 30% of the time a serviceman is always needed. And no matter how short a time you spend, 20% of the time, a serviceman is never needed.

Conclusion:

"What do you suggest?"

We've already spent too much on training – don't let them go down that path.

Key insight: Have a manual that states the first dozen questions all call center operators should ask. The questions should be sufficient to determine if they are in the 30% that always needs a serviceman: if yes, send one while keeping the call as short as possible.

The questions should also be sufficient enough to handle the 20% that never need a serviceman. Those cases should be solved in the most efficient way possible, by the book.

For the rest of the cases, tell the operator to work with the customer on the phone for as long as needed: if they spend over one hour with them on the phone, send a serviceman.

| Case 13: | Jester Motor Company | Difficulty: Hard |

Problem Statement:

"Jester Motors is a major manufacturer of motor vehicles in the US."

Show them Table 1. (See the end of this chapter for the table.) "**What does this table tell you?**" You can give them the following definitions, if they ask:

- CAGR (pronounced "cay-ger"): Compound Annual Growth Rate
- MSRP: Manufacturer's Suggested Retail Price

Key insights that you're looking to hear:

- Total volume remained basically constant over the two year span.
- All vehicle models increased in price with at least 1 increasing about 6% per year on average for two years in a row – a very significant rise.
- Overall, we were able to increase our prices while holding total volume constant, a solid achievement.

Next step:

"How did their revenue change from 2006-2008?"

- Given that Revenue = Price * Volume, and prices and volume increased, total revenue will have also increased annually. The exact revenue depends on the relative quantities of the vehicles we sell. Approximate value could be about 4.2% annually or 8.4% over 2 years. (Prices increased between 0.2% and 6.8% and volume increased 0.6% annually).

"Please fill in the missing luxury car CAGR and minivan's 2008 MSRP value."
For the missing luxury car CAGR:

- The exact value is 6.6%. The formula for calculating CAGRs is:

$$(Year_n / Year_0) \wedge (1/n) -1$$

(If they ask for the formula, it's OK to give it to them.)

- One shortcut for approximating the answer:
  - Round to the nearest thousand and so we're looking for the growth of 49 to 56, which is a change of 7.
  - 7 is 1/7th of 49 so the growth was 1/7th over two years. 1/7=14%.
  - But we want the average annual growth rate, which will be a little less than half the total two year growth rate, or about 7%.

110

For the missing minivan 2008 MSRP value:

- 2006 value was $21,800 with an annual growth rate of 0.5%. This means the two year compound growth rate is a little more than 1.0%. 1.0% of $21,800 is $218, which means the 2008 value is about $22,018. (Using 1.0% for the calculation and $22,000 for the answer is fine).

Next step:

"Let's approximate the luxury car price CAGR at 7%. If it proceeds at that pace, how many years will it take to double in price?"

Answer: About 10 years (using the Rule of 72, $72/7 \approx 10$).

Next step:

Show them Chart 1. **"What does this chart tell you?"**

- Product Mix definition: "Of their total sales, what percentage is each vehicle type".

Key insights that you're looking to hear:

- Given that total volume was about the same in 2006 and 2008, we can say that SUV sales dropped considerably while mid-size and compact car sales increased. All other models' volume stayed constant.

"Overall, were these product mix changes good or bad news for the company?"
Key insights you're looking for:

- While the overall revenue increase is a good sign, we don't have enough information to determine if this is good news. Increasing profitability is our overall objective and so, in addition to revenue, we'd need to see how costs changed during this time to understand the full picture.
- If we assume SUVs have higher margins than other vehicle types (which is usually true), this would be bad news.
- Also, we'd want to know how these figures compare to the market overall. If prices increased for all competitors similarly, then the increase is not a reflection on our efforts. If total industry volume increased during this time, then we have lost market share; if total industry volume decreased, then we gained market share. So overall, more data is needed.

Next step:

"All vehicles priced $30,000 or higher are profitable for us and we lose money on all vehicles priced lower than that, after accounting for fixed costs. The contribution margins per vehicle have remained constant from 2006 to 2008. What does that tell you about our growth in profitability?"

From 2006 to 2008, profitability decreased due to the degradation of product mix. In other words, we're selling more cars that we lose money on (compact and mid-size cars) and selling less that we gain money on (SUVs) while all other models' sales volumes remained constant. (We are assuming that fixed costs remained constant).

"Why are we selling cars that we lose money on?"

Candidate can speculate, but one answer is that those cars have a positive contribution margin but after we subtract fixed costs from them, they become a net loss. Still, they are helping us cover some of our fixed costs and if we sold more of them, they would eventually be profitable. If we stopped selling them, the company overall would lose a lot more money because it couldn't cover its very high fixed costs.

"What can you tell me about how our variable costs per vehicle sold have changed from 2006 to 2008?"

Since we saw growth in prices for all car models, but margins remained constant, we must have also incurred increases in our variable costs for all cars sold.

Next step:

"Let's assume we don't expect SUV sales to turnaround anytime soon. Is there any hope for the company?"

Luxury cars are also profitable and sales are constant. We can either increased their sales or try to make other vehicle types more profitable by increasing prices or decreasing costs.

Conclusion:

"The CEO wants to know your thoughts on how Jester can be more profitable over the next 2 years. What do you suggest?"

We need to sell more cars, especially luxury cars. Candidate can be creative in a few options for doing so.

Case #1 – Sample sheet of notes

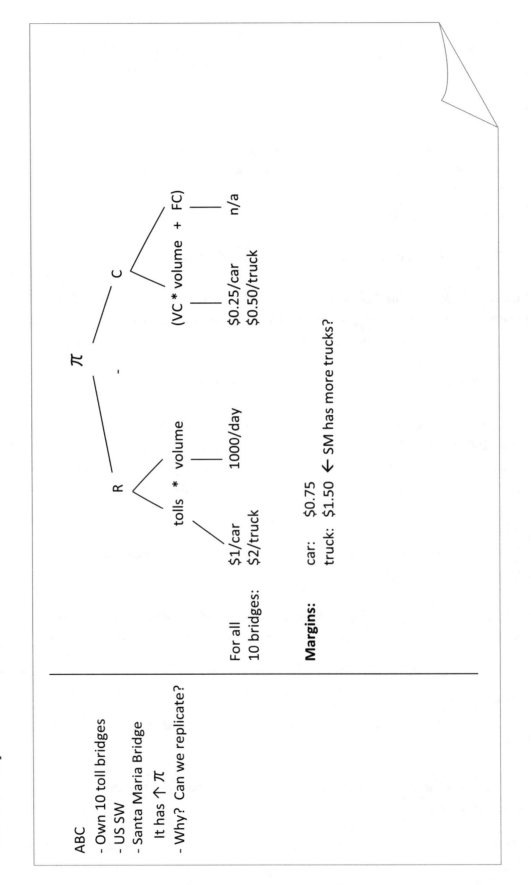

ABC
- Own 10 toll bridges
- US SW
- Santa Maria Bridge
  It has ↑ π
- Why? Can we replicate?

π = R − C

R = tolls * volume
$1/car   1000/day
$2/truck

C = (VC * volume + FC)
$0.25/car   n/a
$0.50/truck

For all
10 bridges:

Margins: car: $0.75
               truck: $1.50 ← SM has more trucks?

Case #4 - Chart 1: US restaurant segmentation by type

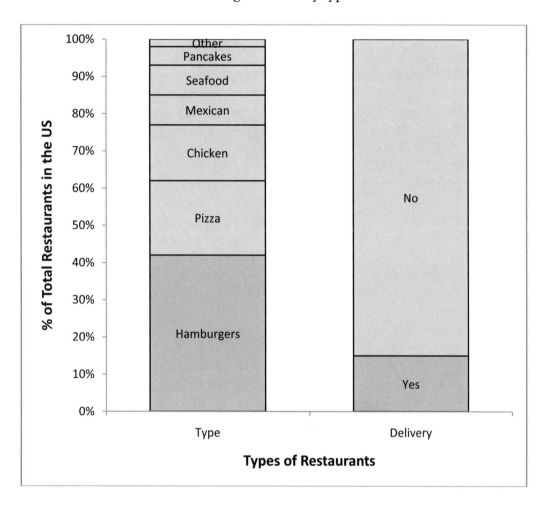

Note: there is no correlation between restaurant type and delivery method.

Case #6 – Table 1: Lemon-AID's financials by product type

Product Group	Revenue (May-June)	Future Growth Potential	Customer Type
Single cup drinks	$150,000	Low	Individuals only
Party packs	$85,000	High	Businesses only
Cookies and snacks	$62,000	High	Individuals and Businesses
T-shirts, etc.	$8,500	Low	Individuals only
Total	$305,500	-	-

Case #6 – Table 2: Segmentation of Lemon-AID's business market

Business Type	Total Spend with Us (per month)	Total Beverage and Snack Spend (per month)
Total of all small businesses in market	$2,500	$34,000
Medium	$25,500	$45,000
Large	$34,500	$67,000
Total	$62,500	$146,000

Case #7 – Chart 1: Profitability per sales type

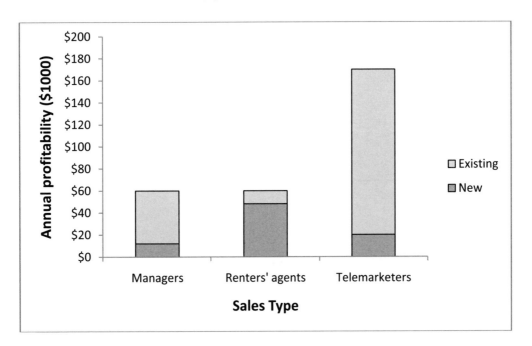

Case #12 – Chart 1: Tech support phone operator effectiveness

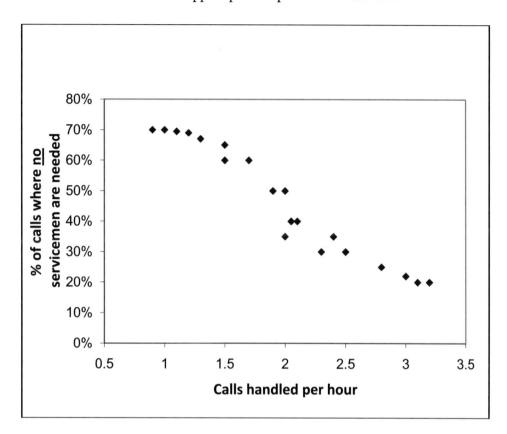

Case #13 – Table 1: Jester Motors' MSRP per product type

	2006	2008	CAGR
Total Volume	3,510,000	3,555,000	0.6%
MSRP (Manufacturer's Suggested Retail Price)			
Compact car	$ 15,000	$ 17,100	6.8%
Mid-size car	$ 21,500	$ 22,800	3.0%
Luxury car	$ 49,300	$ 56,000	___%
Sports car	$ 26,200	$ 26,300	0.2%
Minivan	$ 21,800	_____	0.5%
SUV	$ 30,500	$ 32,500	3.2%
Pickup truck	$ 24,600	$ 25,500	1.8%

Case #13 – Chart 1: Jester Motors' product mix

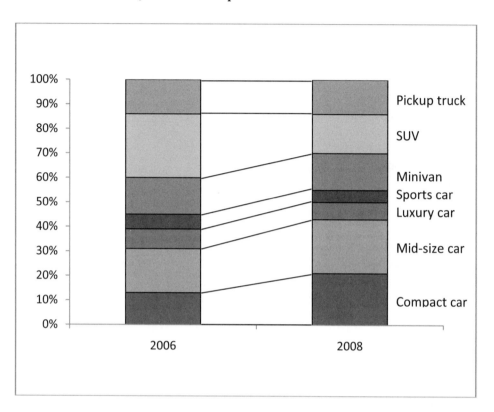

Sample Interview Evaluation Form

0=Did not meet
1=Average
2=Excelled

Past Experience (from résumé and behavioral interview)

    Academics/Intelligence

        School, degree, honors, grades, GMAT

    Achievement

        Leadership

        Facilitated significant change

        Results-oriented

Core skills (from behavioral and case interview)

    Analytics

        Uses structures and frameworks throughout the case

        Can explain the structures they use

        Quantifies issues

        Can test the case issue with data provided

    Communication

        Presenting

        Listening

        Eye contact, posture

        Asks the right questions

        Good in front of the client

Personal (from entire interview)

    Presence

        Enthusiasm

        Team player

        Self-confidence

    Motivation/Interests

        Knows why they want to go into consulting

        Knows why they want to join this specific firm

Total   / 36

Overall assessment (circle one):

    Definite advance   Possible advance   Do not advance

This form may or may not be similar to the evaluation forms that consulting firms use in interviews. It is not meant to represent all of the categories that any of the firms evaluate on.

Appendix 1 – A quick overview of strategy

This section can serve as a quick overview of strategy for candidates that don't have a business or MBA background. In a case interview, you don't need to be an expert on strategy or any other functional area; general problem-solving and communication skills are all you'll need. But case interviews are often about the very high-level, strategic decisions that companies make. A basic knowledge of strategy and how it informs and shapes major business decisions can provide a very helpful backdrop for the popular case interview scenarios.

What is strategy and who sets it?

Strategy is the high-level, 5- to 20-year direction that a company is heading in. Since financial models are usually only viable for a 3-5 year time horizon (if that), strategy ultimately supersedes the planning ability of a mathematical approach in the bigger picture. The CEO often sets a firm's strategy and then the major actions and day-to-day activities of the company should be coordinated to directly support it.

In an organizational chart of a corporation, the scope of the time horizon that any individual plans for is often a function of how high up on the chart they sit. CEOs think about where their company will be in 5-20 years and plan accordingly. VPs of business units plan for up to 5 years in the future. Directors and managers of product lines may plan to a one year budget cycle. And the lowly intern in the mailroom probably only lives his job day by day. Still, while strategy may only be created at the CEO-level, it impacts and sets a context for all of the activities of the rest of the organization.

How do strategy and finance relate?

Most of the case interview suggestions in this book are based in the foundations of finance: the idea that for any decision, we can mathematically calculate the value of it in terms of raw dollars and act only in ways that maximize such value. Therefore you may well ask: if the financial approach is complete and accurate, why do we need to consider "strategy" at all? The answer is that finance and strategy are interrelated.

On the one hand, to create accurate financial valuation models, we require some ability to predict the future: will a new product gain 5% market share in 12 months? Will this acquisition allow us to gain the expected synergies? If we increase our prices to increase our revenue, will we be able to sustain our current sales volume? Simply knowing to ask these questions — let alone answering them with some degree of confidence — requires strategic insights. Strategy gives us the needed perspective and tools to help us balance:

- What we do best
- What our customers want
- How our competitors will act and react   (aka the "3 C's")

On the other hand, creating a strategic goal and meaningfully measuring our progress towards that goal often requires financial measurements and tools. Some of these are discussed throughout this book, especially in relation to the Valuation Framework in Exhibit 6-6.

The types of scenarios posed in case interviews are the big ones that companies may only go through once or twice every few years. These major decisions, such as to launch a new product or acquire a competitor, are ones that can have a significant long-term impact on the direction of the organization. The effects that they have may extend well beyond the 3-5 year financial forecasting period. So at the start of each case, we need to ask why we are considering the action. Does it make sense in terms of our long-term strategy? Will it help us improve our strategic position in the 10-20 year timeframe?

How do you create a strategy?

Harvard Business School professor Michael Porter proposes that companies can only outperform their competitors in the long run if they can create a sustainable point of differentiation either through greater value, lower costs, or both. He writes: "Competitive strategy is about being different... performing *different* activities from rivals' or perform-ing similar activities in *different ways*."[7] This is in contrast to operational effectiveness, which are ways of doing the *same* thing faster, cheaper, or better. Few companies can compete in the long term on the basis of operational effectiveness because all serious competitors quickly share and adopt best practices.

To define a strategy for an organization, the firm must throw its core competencies, its customers' needs, and its competitors' strengths (as well as any other external threats and opportunities) into a mixing bowl and rearrange the pieces until a space is discovered in the market that the firm can own and defend over the long term.

It is unlikely that the details of building a strategy will appear in a case interview, but the more exposure you have to the frameworks of strategy creation, the better the context you'll have for thinking about and discussing the activities that businesses perform.

For more information, Kenichi Ohmae's *The Mind of the Strategist* is a great resource. Michael Porter's books are also industry standard references in the field.

An example of a strategic perspective in a consulting engagement

I recently worked on an engagement for a large non-profit group with a number of locations around the country that assist low-income families.[a] They had developed a software system that they use to standardize and centralize the accounting systems of their member locations. Applying for government grants were previously done using local accounting systems and the move to this standardized system decreased the overhead costs of the local organizations by up to 25%. Given the great results they were able to realize – and the prohibitively high costs for independent non-profits to implement similar systems – they wanted to determine if offering the system to other non-profits could provide a revenue stream for them.

We determined that there were a number of commercialization opportunities, including offering the system over the internet as a subscription model, using it as an acquisition tool, and selling best practices in grant proposals using insights pulled from the database of transactions that they were accumulating. Financial models showed that all of the options could be profitable if they were able to market them effectively to the right audiences. So which one should they focus their attentions on pursuing? One way of thinking about answering that question is to consider what they wanted to be ten years in the future. When they imagined how others would describe themselves years in the future, was it as "a unified collection of local non-profits that use funding resources more effectively than any similar sized peer"? Or was it as "a unified collection of local non-profits and a technology solutions provider"? Even before many of the strategic perspectives in Ohmae and Porter's books can be applied, a simple question needs to be asked: "what is the business that we're in?" Simple as it may seem, it can be complex and valuable process for an organization to reflect on that question before making any major new investment.

As one example, on February 5, 2009, the Wall Street Journal reported that Procter & Gamble announced plans to open a national chain of car wash franchises. Does doing so allow it to make incremental progress towards a larger future strategic end goal, such as to be a national leader in the service industry? Or is this just an experiment that will simply dilute its leadership's attention from its core business of selling household products? Only time will tell, but the business news is full of similar stories to consider.

In the case of my previous client, considering where they wanted to end up in the distant future really helped them determine how to set up and move their chess pieces in the near term. Ultimately, they may never arrive at the substantial end goal that they aligned themselves to, but it was a valuable frame of reference to know that if they achieve success in their near-term activities, those successes could compound and allow them to reach an otherwise unimaginable destination. Companies often have multiple options that promise high profitable rewards and having a strategic direction can help filter them out.

---

[a] The nature of client's industry and the details of the engagement have been changed.

Companies have to choose actions that coordinate; they can't do everything in every industry. These coordinated actions, despite being profitable, also help to strengthen the overall position of the organization in ways that are greater than the sum of its parts.

Exhibit A-1 shows the "Three Horizons" framework, as developed by McKinsey & Company. It can be used to visualize how near-term activities tie to long-term strategic goals.

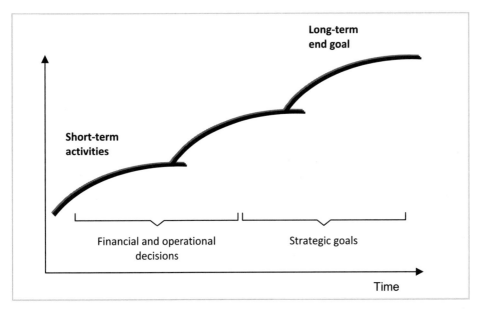

Exhibit A-1 The Three Horizons framework links short-term activities to long-term strategic goals

To tie it back to the earlier discussion of the company's organization chart, CEOs and other top leaders are the visionaries that should be imagining the possible long-term future state and reinforcing the overall mission statement to build alignment towards it. Managers and directors make use of deep functional expertise to drive performance in the short-term activities. In the middle are the VPs that manage uncertainty in the middle-term and fund and encourage new ventures and risk-taking to develop the new opportunities. Short-term activities should keep the company healthy while middle-term ventures should build on the present successes and allow the firm to keep its options open on the range of future strategic goals that the leaders envision.

What does all of this mean for case interviews? While we should take a financial approach when determining whether a firm should introduce a new product or acquire a competitor, we should ask upfront how the proposed action aligns with the firm's strategic direction. Granted, any acquisition or new product could be divested a few years later after generating additions to the bottom line, but while doing so it could become a sinkhole of the leadership's time and energy. Major moves out of step with a strategic goal can obscure the firm's overall mission in the minds of its employees and shareholders who are looking for direction in the shorter-term arcs on the horizon.

Appendix 2 – A quick overview of valuation details

For the purposes of case interviews, the simplifications that we've made so far are reasonable and meaningful. But there are some details needed to fully explain the connection between "Profits" and "Value of target" / "Value of product" in the Valuation Framework in Exhibit 6-6.

First, we can consider the standalone value of a product or target company to be the net present value (NPV) of all its future profits. More precisely, though, the standalone value is the NPV of all future free cash flows (FCFs) created by a product or business. FCFs are the annual post-tax operating profits after deducting the continual capital re-investment costs that are needed to grow the business.

Additionally, when valuing companies (as we do for mergers and acquisitions), we should make further clarification: while companies are owned by both equity holders and debt holders, only equity holders have a claim to the increased potential future profits of a firm. Therefore to acquire a target in the hopes of gaining value through synergies, you only need to purchase its equity. So we need to subtract the value of the debt from the standalone value of the firm when calculating the value of a possible acquisition.

the standalone value of a firm   = standalone value of its equity + value of its debt
                                     = the NPV of FCFs (free cash flows)

Therefore,

the standalone value of a target's equity = NPV of FCFs - the value of its debt

Again, this level of detail is not needed for case interviews. But conceivably, you could explain the dotted line between "value of target" and "profits" in Exhibit 6-6 as: "The value of the target to its shareholders is a direct function of its expected future profitability. Specifically, the value is the NPV of all future post-tax profits *minus* the annual amount needed to be reinvested to grow and maintain the business *minus* the value held by its debtholders."

Index

Bibliography and References

- Cosentino, M. (2005). *Case In Point: Complete Case Interview Preparation - Fourth edition.* Needham, MA: Burgee Press.
- Greenleaf, R. (1977). *Servant Leadership.* Mahwah, NJ: Paulist Press.
- Koller, T., M. Goedhart, D. Wessels, T. Copeland. (2005). *Valuation: Measuring and Managing the Value of Companies - Fourth edition.* Hoboken, NJ: John Wiley & Sons, Inc.
- Marn, M., E. Roegner, and C. Zawada. (2004). *The Price Advantage.* New York: John Wiley & Sons Australia, Limited.
- Minto, B. (1996). *The Minto Pyramid Principle: Logic in Writing, Thinking and Problem Solving.* London: Minto International.
- Ohmae, K. (1982). *The Mind of the Strategist.* New York: McGraw-Hill, Inc.
- Porter, M. (1985). *Competitive Advantage.* New York: Free Press.
- Porter, M. (1980). *Competitive Strategy.* New York: Free Press.
- Porter, M. (1996). "What is Strategy?" *Harvard Business Review.* November-December, 1996.
- Welch, J. and J. Byrne. (2001). *Jack: Straight from the Gut.* New York: Warner Business Books.

Acknowledgements

Thanks to Adam Jenkins, who spent many hours helping me prepare for my case interviews.

Thanks to the many people contributed ideas and corrections, especially: Oleg Bestsennyy, Amit Bhardwaj, Kfir Catalan, Marc Cosentino, Jasmeet Dhall, Parag Gupta, Pawan Kapoor, Sachin Kotwani, Sachal Lakhavani, Jim and Kelley Mavros, my parents, Matt Rhenish, Jainik Shah, Eric Silver, Balika Sonthalia, Josh Swartz, Zeynep Tolon, Charles Tsang, Jesse Wu, and Jiang Xin.

About the cover

The golden ratio, 1.618…, appears in the main elements of this book's cover multiple times. The ratio of the height of the top red and white bands to the bottom red one is 1.6:1. Within the top two bands, the same is true for the heights of the white one to the red one. The ratio of the man's arm to his torso is 1.6:1. And the author's name is centered 2.5" down in a 4.1" high red block: 2.5:1.6 is also a ratio of 1.6:1.

---

[1] Marn, M., et al. (2004). Page 5.

[2] Marn, M., et al. (2004). Pages 44-56.

[3] Koller, T., et al. (2005). Page 435.

[4] Koller, T., et al. (2005) Pages 441-442.

[5] Ohmae, K. (1982). Pages 91-92.

[6] Welch, J. (2001). Page 392.

[7] Porter, M. (1996). Page 61-78. [Italics are his.]